400 STORY SEEDS TO CRUSH WRITER'S BLOCK

Written By
M. Kirin

Edited By
Kitty Lynn

Cover Art By
PLAGUESWORTH

400 Story Seeds to Crush Writer's Block

ISBN-10: 194053707X
ISBN-13: 978-1-940537-07-8

TABLE OF CONTENTS

FOREWORD

Hello there,

My name is M. Kirin, and I started a writing advice blog back in 2012. Over the years, I've gotten thousands of questions and emails regarding just about everything in the author world.

So. What do you think is the number one question I've received over the years? It goes a little something like this:

What is 'Writer's Block?' Some authors like to argue that it doesn't exist, but I think differently. Writer's Block has more to do with an author's thoughts on themselves than their methods. I believe Writer's Block is the fear of facing judgement and the doubt of one's talents. I've faced these problems in the past, much like any other author out there. I've been afraid of what people would think of me because of my writing, and I've doubted my ability to come up with an original idea. As you can tell, these are very personal problems, and the answer needs to come from the self.

Now, although I'm known for being a rather nosey person on the internet, I don't think that the correct way to fix Writer's Block is to give therapy to each individual writer in the world. Again, personal problems are most effectively solved by the self. I've always believed that the best learning is done by doing. So, my goal was set.

Instead of just telling people they could overcome this obstacle, I realized I needed something that could prove — by the very act of writing — that yes, you are indeed able to overcome Writer's Block.

I call them *Story Seeds*.

What's a Story Seed? It's a little bundle of ideas and questions to get your mind thinking. It's a set of parameters to kick your imagination into over-drive. A Story Seed may come with characters, locations, objects, situations, or all of the above. It's up to you to fill-in the blanks, to connect the dots, and find the story that only you could tell. Thousands of people may look at the same Seed, and they will all come up with an entirely different story. Heck— the same person could look at the same Seed many times and write dozens of books.

That's the magic of Story Seeds.

This is my cure for Writer's Block. What better way to dissolve fear and doubt than to show a writer that (yes!) you can write anything you want and that (yes!) you hold inside of you countless stories.

I think there's nothing quite as empowering as realizing that you hold inside of yourself an endless well of imagination: characters, locations, objects, and situations that you — and only you — could've come up with.

What do you get with this book? 400 Story Seeds. 400 ideas to get your imagination rolling. 400 launchpads to get you writing. Some of them come with pieces you get to play with, and others will ask you to make the pieces yourself. There is no right or wrong. Each story you come up with is perfect, uniquely yours, and if you dedicate yourself to it (and give it a little love), it will bloom into something only you could've made.

The Story Seeds in this book are separated into four categories, depending on what sort of story you feel like telling. I believe that all stories are ultimately about characters, but they all don't start like that. A character who decides to run away from their home is different from one who was drafted into a war. The places we live in, the things we interact with, and the situations we find ourselves in change us. That's why the Story Seeds in this book are broken down into four groups:

*001 - 100 are Story Seeds that start with **Character**.*
*101 - 200 are Story Seeds that start with **Locations**.*
*201 - 300 are Story Seeds that start with **Objects**.*
*301 - 400 are Story Seeds that start with **Situations**.*

As an added bonus, you will find that the first Story Seed in each mini-category will be more open-ended and less complex. For example, #081 "The Best-Selling Author" is a lot more open than #084 "Pretty Penny," even if they both deal with a similar scenario. With that in mind, please remember the following:

Story Seeds are not prompts or writing exercises. You will not be graded on them or asked if you learned the 'lesson.' You bought this book, these 400 Seeds are

yours. Play with them. Change them. Twist them. Do whatever you need to do to tell the story.

There is no right or wrong. There are only the stories you **write** and those you **don't**.

The best learning can only be done by doing. You can read all the books in the world about gardening, but you don't know a thing until you get your hands dirty.

So, grab a Story Seed and get writing!

— M. Kirin

001 - 100

Story Seeds that start with
CHARACTERS

*"Nearly all men can stand adversity,
but if you want to test a man's
character, give him power."*

Abraham Lincoln

001 - 004

Whether it's changing schools, starting a new job, or being introduced to a new circle of friends — there's always conflict that comes with transition. It may not be an external conflict, like getting in a fight with the new boss; it may also be internal, like feeling hopeless at the prospect of having to start over from zero, yet again.

001
The New Kid

Write about a character who finds themselves in a new place (school, work, home, etc.). Explore their feelings as they try to adapt to this change. How did this character end up in this new place? Did this character like the place they came from, or is this 'change' just the latest step in a downwards spiral?

002
Too Good to be True?

Write about a character who finds themselves in a new place and soon realize that there's something there that makes them unbelievably happy. What did they find? Is this enough to undo the frustration of starting over from zero? Or... could it be it's too good to be true?

003
You're Looking at it the Wrong Way

Write about a character who finds themselves in a new place, but they perceive everything around them differently than it really is. Is this character looking at the downside of everything, or are they sugarcoating it all? Why has this character resorted to looking at the world differently than it really is? Could it be... that this character is not even aware they're doing it?

004
The New Kid, Reversed

Write about a character who is tasked with showing the place to the newest arrival. Does this character welcome the newcomer, or is this character too busy with their own problems? Was there a time when this character was new to the place they're showing off? What is the *one* thing the newcomer wants to know, but that this character is not going to tell them?

005 - 008

In every social gathering, there's always the one person who is not talking. It's not because they can't — but because they choose not to. They may not express it, but there's a reason behind this choice. There always is.

005
The Silent One

Write about a character who finds themselves at a social gathering but chooses to remain silent at all times. Explore the thoughts that this character cannot voice. Why did this character go to that gathering in the first place? How are the people around them reacting to their silence? And what's keeping this character at the gathering — why don't they just leave?

006
Why So Serious?

Write about a character who finds themselves at a social gathering but chooses to remain silent at all times... except that this character isn't shy, but terrified. What did this character see, or experience, that has them so spooked? If there was reason to worry, this character would let everyone know, right? Or could it be that the source of this character's terror is standing right before them?

007
Is Everyone Okay?

Write about a character who finds themselves at a social gathering, but soon discovers that no one around them is talking. What's the first thing that this character notices as they enter the gathering? Why is everyone silent? Is there reason to be afraid? Could it be that they all know something this character doesn't?

008
That's What Friends are For

Write about a character who finds themselves at a social gathering, and notice that one of their friends is very quiet. Does this character know what's wrong with their friend? Are they willing to go over to them and help, or does this character has problems of their own? What would happen if this character was willing to help their friend, but only because of an ulterior motive?

009 - 012

In every social gathering, there's always the one person who is not talking. It's not because they can't — but because they choose not to. They may not express it, but there's a reason behind this choice. There always is.

009
The Overprotective Sibling

Write about a character who is extremely overprotective of their sibling. Has this character always been like this, or did something happen in the past that made them like that? Where does this character draw the line? Would they be willing to hurt their sibling to keep them 'safe?' How do they rationalize their actions? They must surely have a reason to act like this; they don't see themselves as tyrants... right?

010
We're Too Old For This

Write about a character who is extremely overprotective of their sibling, except that these characters are old enough to have families of their own. Why is this character so overprotective, even at an older age? How does the sibling's family feel about this character's actions? Why has this character dedicated their life to protecting their sibling— do they not have dreams or a family of their own? Could it be this character has nothing left... but their sibling?

011
History Repeats Itself

Write about a character who is extremely overprotective of their sibling, except that they only do so when their sibling does *something*. What is their sibling doing, and why does this character feel that they need to protect them? What's more dangerous, the thing the sibling is doing or this character's overprotective nature? And why has this sibling continued to repeat the same cycle, even if they know this character is going to try and stop them?

012
I Can't Lose You Again

Write about a character who is so overprotective of their sibling that they're borderline *abusive*— except they think they have a good reason for being so. Explore the history between this character and their sibling. Does this character believe they're abusive? Was there a time when they were not so overprotective? And, worst of all, how would this character change if their sibling... died?

013 - 016

Some of us hide our emotions behind lies and others behind actions. It could be as insignificant as biting our nails whenever we are stressed or as strange as... laughing in the most awkward of situations.

013
The Hyena

Write about a character who masks their real emotions behind laughter. Has this character always been like this, or did something happen in their past that changed them? How do 'normal' people react to this character? Does anyone around them realize that their laughter is nothing but a mask? And did this character make this 'mask' on their own, or did someone teach them to hide their fears behind laughter?

014
Not All Jokes End with a Punch Line

Write about a character who masks their real emotions behind laughter, as they find themselves in a place where laughing would get them in trouble. How do the people around this character react? What is making this character laugh, and why can't they force themselves to stop? Who is truly the one in control: the mask or the character?

015

I Laugh in the Face of Death

Write about a character who masks their real emotions behind laughter, and they're convinced that this doesn't make them weak— but *strong*. How did they come to this conclusion? Does this truly make them stronger? And, worst of all, what would be the greatest test to this so-called 'strength?'

016

Laughter is the Greatest Medicine

Write about a character who masks their real emotions behind laughter. As odd as it may seem, this character actually manages to help another person with their laughter. Explore this moment, along with the thoughts of this character. Can laughter really be the greatest medicine, or is it just a temporary cure?

017 - 020

We all have people we look up to, and in our eyes, they not only represent human excellence but our hopes for a better future. After all, if they could achieve greatness, then we should be able to do the same, right? But... what if they're not what they seem? What if their trophies were not earned – but bought?

017
The False Champion

Write about a character who is considered an example of human excellence, except that in reality they're nothing like it. Did this character choose to be a 'fake,' or were they simply a victim of happenstance? Explore the thoughts of this character as they reflect on their past... and their future. They say liars don't prosper, but is this true? Does this character, this liar, want to prosper? What does your character think is the true price of living a lie?

018
Denial Cast in Gold

Write about a character who is considered an example of human excellence, except that in reality, they're nothing like it. Additionally, although this character is living a lie, they also believe that they're doing the 'right' thing. How could this possibly be true? Explore the events of the past, along with the effects they had on this character. How could a lie be better than the truth?

019
You Say You Hate it and Yet

Write about a character who is considered an example of human excellence, except that in reality, they're nothing like it. Additionally, this character shows extreme anger and bitterness at the idea of being considered a 'champion'… and yet they choose to continue living a lie. Explore the duality of this character. How can they enjoy the benefits of the lie and yet, at the same time, despise it?

020
You Can Lie to the World, but Not Me

Write about a character, seemingly the only person in the world, who believes a champion of human excellence is living a lie. How has this character come to this conclusion? What's their relationship with this 'champion;' do they know each other from years prior? If this character had the chance to reveal the truth to the world, would they do it? Would the world really benefit from losing their example of human excellence, even if it is a lie?

021 - 024

What if there was a person who seemed adult in appearance, and yet, they held inside of them the untarnished – perfect, flawless – curiosity and joy of youth? Would this person be better off, or would they be trampled by the realities of being an adult?

021
The Eternal Child

Write about a character who never 'grew up.' Explore their everyday life, along with their thoughts on the world around them. How has this character survived being an 'adult?' Was there ever a time when this character was not so innocent and child-like? How do other people react around this character? And, above all, how does this character react to facing the harsh reality that they may need to 'grow up?'

022
Invincible Summer

Write about a character who never 'grew up,' and yet they are a fully functional adult. Explore the thoughts of this character as they reflect overcoming the challenges of 'adulthood' without ever losing their inner-child. Is their lifestyle healthy— and is it effective? Was there anyone in the past who encouraged them to hold on to their inner-child? And, most importantly, what would be the greatest test of this character's lifestyle?

023
The Mask that Couldn't Fool Time

Write about a character who hides their real emotions by acting immaturely. What happened to this character; how has this become their defense-mechanism from their own emotions? Do they have anyone around them who knows the truth? And, above all, is this 'mask' effective— does it really protect them, or is it only a matter of time before they have to face the truth?

024
A New Way

Write about a character who stumbles upon a person who behaves nothing like their age. How does this character react to meeting this odd person? Is this character at all jealous of the freedom with which this person expresses themselves? And, most importantly, what does this character see when they look at that odd person? Is that a new way of life or a ticking time-bomb?

025 - 028

Where does fear come from? Is it something we are born with, or do we develop fears depending on our circumstances? What if we encountered someone who was afraid – terribly afraid – of something that to the rest of us may seem… harmless?

025

The Fearful One

Write about a character who is terrified by something mundane. Was this character born with this fear, or did they develop it over time? Have they reached out for professional help in the past; if so— did it help? What adjustments have they made to their everyday life in order to protect themselves from this fear? What would this character do if they found themselves all alone surrounded by nothing but… the object of their fear?

026

Courage Seems So Far Away

Write about a character who is terrified by something mundane, but thanks to the words of someone dear to them, they're inspired to try to overcome it. Who was the person who tried to help them, and what did they tell this character that was so effective? Explore the thoughts of this character as they attempt to overcome their fear. Pit extreme courage against extreme terror. Which is victorious: this character or the fear?

027

You Should be Afraid Too

Write about a character who has a very good reason for being afraid. There is something horrible going on, and they know that if the people around them found out, they would lose their minds. What could this 'horrible' thing be? Is the whole world in danger? And, above all, what reasons does this character have for hiding the truth?

028

Is It... Contagious?

Write about a character who is friends with a very fearful person. What are the differences between this character and their friend? What about the similarities? What does this character think about their friend's fearful nature? What would they do if they realized that, little by little, they've started developing the same fears?

029 - 032

In our lives we all experience love, whether it is the love of one's parents, love of one's country, or – of course – love of another person. But unfortunately, not all love lasts. For every 'happily ever after,' there are countless broken hearts.

029

The Destroyed Heart

Write about a character who has faced heartbreak so great they believe they will never love anyone ever again. What happened to this character? Was it something as petty as a break-up... or did Death play a part in it? Do people around this character understand their pain, and are they supportive or belittling? And, most importantly, does this character *truly* believe that they may never love again?

030

Queen of Hearts

Write about a character who has faced heartbreak so great they believe they will never love anyone ever again... except that one day, this character finds themselves face-to-face with the person who 'destroyed' their heart. How does this character react? Does this encounter give the character a chance to repair their heart, or does it leave them even more hurt than before?

031

You Weren't the Only One Hurt

Write about a character who is told that they broke someone's heart. What was this character's relationship with the other person? How does this character feel about the claims? Did they really break the other person's heart… or could it be that both hearts were broken? What would this character say if they had a chance to meet with the person who has been pushing these claims?

032

No One is Alone

Write about a character who is secretly in love with one of their closest friends and desperately wants to reveal their feelings… except their friend has recently faced great heartbreak. Does this character feel they are better off keeping their feelings to themselves— or is this the time to finally declare their love? Explore the thoughts and feelings of this character as they find themselves alone with their friend. It may not be the perfect time to reveal their feelings… but will there *ever* be a perfect time and place?

033 - 036

Life is unfair. It not only wounds us terribly; it also leaves behind scars that will forever remind us of our mistakes and our failures. But... scars are not only reminders of the past, they're stories written on our flesh.

033
The Scarred One

Write about a character who is scarred. What is the story behind their scar? Does this character attempt to hide it from the world? How do other people react to this character's scar? Explore the mind of a character who wears on their flesh an eternal reminder of their past. And, most importantly, if someone were to approach and ask where the scar came from... would this character be open to share the story?

034
Except Not

Write about a character who is scarred... except that whenever asked for the story behind the scar, they lie about it. What's the real story behind the scar? Why would this character hide the truth? Are they trying to protect their 'honor,' or are they trying to hide something much worse? And, above all, what would this character do if someone dear to them asked to hear the 'real' story behind the scar?

035
An Unlikely Match

Write about a character who is scarred... and just so happens to stumble upon a person who sports a scar identical to theirs. What is the first thing this character does when they realize the similarities? Does the other person notice the same? Does this character have the courage to approach the other person and ask how they got their scar? Could it be that it's all just happenstance... or is it possible that their scars share more than just appearance?

036
Invisible Sadness

Write about a character who is scarred... except their scar is not physical but emotional. Something hurt this character so deeply that they now carry an invisible brand on their heart— what could've possibly done this? Does anyone know what this character is going through? Would anyone be brave enough to try and help, or is this character alone in their suffering? What would this character do if someone approached them and offered to help them?

037 - 040

037

The Invincible Heart

Write about a character who always overcomes every challenge they face, and although things may look grim sometimes, they never lose their optimism. Does this character have friends? If so, how do they feel about this character's invincible nature? Has this character's ability to overcome adversity earned them fame? Does anyone look up to this character? What is the real story behind this character; are they truly blessed, or do they know something everyone else doesn't?

038

Kryptonite

Write about a character who always overcomes every challenge they face... except for one thing. There is *something* that can break this character's invincible heart— what is it? Is it something mundane or something much darker? Is this something the character keeps secret from the world? What would this character do if the only way to save the life of someone dear to them was to face the only thing they're unable to overcome?

039

Snake Eyes

Write about a character who always overcomes every challenge they face... except that, for some strange reason, they appear to have *awful* luck. They overcome adversity, but just barely. This character is getting by, surviving, but earning no fame or fortune along the way. How does this character feel about this? Do they find peace in knowing that they lead a safe life— or do they desire for more than just safety? Is there anything this character can do to change their luck?

040

Devil's Advocate

Write about a character who believes a person close to them is hiding something. The person in question appears to overcome all adversity with relative ease— to the point that this character is certain that something strange is going on. When did this character first begin to doubt this person? Has this character told anyone about their suspicions? What would this character do if they found themselves alone in a room with this person?

041 - 044

Books, movies, music; they all serve as momentary distractions from our daily lives. Escapism is healthy… but what happens when it is taken to an extreme? What if your only escape from life was to daydream?

041
The Daydreamer

Write about a character who spends most of their time daydreaming. Explore their mind — or rather their daydreams — as they try to escape their life. Has this character always been like this? What is their earliest memory of them daydreaming to escape? How does this character rationalize their daydreams to people around them? What does their dream world look like? And, above all, what exactly is this character's reason for escaping into the dream world?

042
Mirror World

Write about a character who spends most of their time daydreaming… except that, after suffering a terrible accident, this character returns to their dream world to find that everything has changed. What happened to this character's dream world? Does the change in the dream world reflect the change the accident caused… or could it be that the two are not connected at all? What would this character do if they realized the place they used to escape to has changed for the worst?

043
You're (Not) Alone

Write about a character who spends most of their time daydreaming... except that they're not the only ones. Their closest friend also happens to be a daydreamer. How did they originally meet? Did they know at once that they had found someone like them, or did it take a great event for them to see the similarities? What would this character do if their friend suddenly stopped daydreaming? Is it a time to change, or a time to find a new friend?

044
Follow the White Rabbit

Write about a character who spends most of their time daydreaming... except that they truly believe their dream world is a real place. When did this character first start believing this? Have they ever dared to tell anyone around them? Could it be true; is this dream world a real place or merely hallucinations? What would this character do if one day, the dream world began to spill into the 'real' world?

045 - 048

Libraries are a sanctuary for books and those who love to read them. But what if the gatekeeper to this place was a little odd? Actually, more than just a little odd.

045

The Librarian

Write about the strangest librarian you can think of. How exactly are they strange? Is it their appearance, behavior, or both? What is the first thing anyone would notice about this library and the person who runs it? Is the exterior world at all aware of their strangeness, or would a person have to stop and look for a while in order to see that there was something a little odd about this librarian? Actually, more than just a *little* odd.

046

A Taste for Fiction

Write about a strange librarian who only likes one genre, book type, or writing style, to the extreme that they only stock these books. What is the reason behind their obsession with these types of books? Is this librarian open to conversation about that? How has these changes affected the library? And, above all, how do the people who frequent this library feel?

047
A Librarian Only in Name

Write about a character who is supposed to be a librarian, but they're not very good at it. What is this character failing at? Are they at all interested in improving— or do they not care? How is it that they can keep their job while being so bad at it? What would this character do if they heard the county was looking to replace them with a more competent librarian? Is this the 'out' they've been waiting for or quite the contrary?

048
Describe What You Saw, Please

Write about a character who is trying to describe the strange librarian they encountered hours prior to someone. What exactly happened between this character and the strange librarian? Who is this character talking to: the police, a close friend… or someone they've never seen before? What exactly happened to this character? And what did the strange librarian do that not even this character can believe?

049 - 052

Fame can't be all glitter and gold — even celebrities have bad days, sad days, or just... boring days. Between award ceremonies, dinner parties, and being the target of paparazzi, there has got to be a mundane moment somewhere, right?

049
The Celebrity

Write about a character who happens to be a celebrity. How has fame and fortune changed this character's life? When was the last time this character felt like a 'normal' person? Do they miss it? Do they find pride in living in fame, or do they regret not being able to walk the streets without a bodyguard? What does this character think to themselves when they look down at the crowds from their penthouse window?

050
I Would Rather Stay in the Castle

Write about a character who happens to be a celebrity, except they never leave their home because they're tired of dealing with rabid fans and paparazzi. How does this character feel about this change in lifestyle? What would this character do if they saw someone outside who desperately needed their help? Is this character willing to walk out of their home and help this stranger— knowing that the media will spin and twist the story regardless of what this character does?

051

I Don't Know Any Better

Write about a character who happens to be a celebrity, except that they've been famous since they were very young. How has this lifestyle changed this character's perception of 'regular' life? Do they romanticize being a normal person or spit on the faces of anyone who doesn't respect them? After all, they've *earned* their fortune and fame, right? What would this character do if they found themselves in a place where their name and their money meant nothing?

052

Stars Against Suns

Write about a character who happens to be a celebrity as they stumble upon another celebrity— one they're *huge* fans of. How does the character react to this encounter? Do they keep their cool, or do they find themselves acting like the rabid fans they hate? How would this character react if they discovered that the celebrity they adore felt the same way about them?

053 - 056

There is a profession that gets no slack whatsoever: politicians. And with good reason. There is plenty of proof that some people with the legislative power to create change for the better would rather fill their pockets with gold. But... are they all bad? Could it be that there's maybe an angel or two amongst the suited devils?

053
The Politician

Write about a character who happens to be a politician. Explore the duality of having the power to change the world, along with carrying the weight of duty. How did this character decide to become a politician? Is this character extremely passionate about their job— or are they just in it for the paycheck? What would this character do if they were offered a substantial sum of money in exchange for supporting a political issue that contradicts their values?

054
I'm Not a Crook

Write about a character who happens to be a politician, except that they've recently come under fire by the media. What is this character accused of doing? Is there anyone who still trusts this character— or have they been abandoned by everyone they knew? What does this character do when they're told they have to admit to the claims of the media— regardless of whether they are true or not?

055
I Believe in Harvey Dent

Write about a character who happens to be a politician, and during their career, they have become a source of inspiration to a lot of people. How does this character feel about this? Do they believe they've earned the trust of the people, or do they believe they're a fake? Is this character hiding something— and if they are, how long do they think they have before everyone finds out they're nothing more than a lie?

056
Played by Kevin Spacey

Write about a character who happens to be a politician, except they play by their own rules. They do whatever they want and manage to achieve their goals with very little consequences. Everyone who stands up against them is either found dead within hours or simply end up siding with this character. Explore the origins of this character. Are they really just *that* charismatic... or is there something else going on underneath the surface? What would this character do if they came face-to-face with the most powerful person in the country— have they finally found their match or quite the contrary?

057 - 060

Even if it's just trading cards, in the eye of The Collector, this item is more than just a piece of paper — it's the one thing they never had, and now they're able to gather it with abandon.

057
The Collector

Write about a character who happens to be a collector. What item does this character like to collect? What do these items mean to them? What is their earliest memory of encountering these items? Explore the thoughts of this character as they make the decision to reduce the money they spend on food so that they can buy another item for their collection. How do they rationalize doing this? What does this character do when they start to feel hungry — is their collection truly worth such a sacrifice?

058
The Final Piece

Write about a character who happens to be a collector, as they finally gather the last item needed to complete their collection. What items has this character been collecting? For how long has this character been looking for the last item? Is there anything they sacrificed in order to obtain it? How does this character feel when they finally complete their collection? Is that relief in their eyes... or despair?

059
The World Needs My Collection

Write about a character who happens to be a collector. Although their collection may seem mundane, it is actually crucial to the survival of mankind. What is this character collecting? Does the world know that their fate is in the hands of someone's personal collection? What would happen if, one day, this character realized that someone has vandalized their collection? Is the world doomed... or is there still hope?

060
Prepare to Die Edition

Write about a character who happens to be a collector, except that their collection is rather *gruesome*. What does this character collect? How did they develop this obsession with these particular objects? Is this 'collection' something the world is aware of, or is this character less of a collector and more of a... serial killer?

061 - 064

Selfish or selfless; it doesn't matter. Robbing from the rich or from the poor; it doesn't matter. The question is: "How did they end up like this?" Normal people don't end up robbing banks. Along the path of life, we are given options; no one is 'really' born a thief... right?

061

The Thief

Write about a character who happens to be a thief. Explore not what they steal, but why they choose to take from others. How does this character rationalize stealing? Do they feel any sense of guilt, or do they simply shrug their shoulders and say that life is unfair? Where does this character draw the line? And, most importantly, would they be willing to steal from someone who is worse off than them?

062

My Sister's Child Was Close to Death

Write about a character who entered a life of thievery to help their family... except that Lady Luck has not been kind to this character. For every item they steal, something else goes wrong. Explore the thoughts of this character as they realize they're caught in a downwards spiral. Does this character have hope that things will get better? Would this character be willing to leave their family if it also means they would be able to leave their life of thievery?

063

All Crimes are the Same

Write about a character who sees no difference between killing and stealing and commits both crimes with abandon. Has this character always been like this, or did something happen in the past that changed them? How does this character rationalize putting their life and needs before everyone else's? What would this character do if their contractor offered them money to kill a child?

064

Single Exception

Write about a character who happens to be a thief. For a price, this character is willing to steal anything— except *one* thing. What sort of item is this character not willing to steal? Does this character have a history with this type of item? What would this character do if they were approached by a strange person, who offered them a ludicrous amount of money, enough so that this character would never have to steal again, in exchange for stealing this item? They say that everything has a price, even a person's morals, but is this true?

065 - 068

They travel great distances to see firsthand the different facets of our world. To The Foreigner, their greatest enemy is language – but they are willing to face this challenge because they're curious. They travel in search of the truth that there has to be more to our planet than their hometown, more ways to live than to work at the family farm.

065
The Foreigner

Write about a character who is a foreigner in strange lands. Why did this character set out in the first place? Why would they be so willing to leave everything and everyone they knew behind? Explore the inner conflict of this character. What are they most afraid of: death in the face of such strange lands or a realization that they may never find a place to call 'home?' And, above all, if they find the journey so hard… why don't they just turn around and go back where they came from?

066
Citizen of Planet Earth

Write about a character who has been traveling the world since they were little. They know lots of languages and have experienced lots of cultures. How has seeing the world changed them? How does this character look at people who have never left their hometown? Is there a place this character considers their home, or has a life of seeing the world taken from them the ability to settle anywhere?

067

Homesick

Write about a character who is a foreigner in strange lands, and while traveling, they can't help but think about their family back home. Everything this character comes in contact with reminds them of their homeland. Is this character truly homesick, or is it something else they're afraid of? If they long to be home and miss their family, why don't they just go back? Could it be that… 'home' doesn't exist anymore?

068

No Se Aceptan Extranjeros

Write about a character who is a foreigner in strange lands, except that they do not speak the native language and their phrase-book is nowhere to be found. What is this character's first reaction when they realize that they have lost all means of communicating with the locals? How does this character plan to continue their journey? What would this character do if they realized that they've gotten in trouble with the locals? How could this character get themselves out of this dilemma?

069 - 072

The greatest struggle of any artist is having to choose between making art or making rent. Society praises art in all of its forms, and yet, it shows no pity to the artists scrounging to pay their bills.

069
The Starving Artist

Write about a character who is a master of their craft, and yet, they're hardly getting by. Explore the duality of someone who is amazing at their art, but also finds that it's not sufficient to support them. How does this character's friends, family, and loved ones feel about the pursuit of their art? Where does this character draw their courage from? Why do they keep making their art when they know that the bills are pilling up? If they were given a chance, would this character be willing to let go of their art in exchange for the money to get by— or would they rather starve?

070
All the Wrong Reasons

Write about a character who is a master of their craft, and yet, they're hardly getting by. What happens to this character when a strange person approaches them, offering them an enormous sum of money for their art? Except, there's a catch: the world will never know this character's name. What does this character do? Would they be willing to accept the wealth without any of the recognition?

071

Hard Choices

Write about a character who is a master of their craft and also has a family to feed. Their art is not bringing in enough money, and it's only a matter of time before they're so far in debt that they can't get out. Of course, the easiest option is to give up their art. Explore the thoughts and fears of this character as they try to find other options instead of letting go of their art. There has to be another way... right?

072

Not a Master, but an Apprentice

Write about a character who is new to their craft. They may be young or just starting up— but the struggle is the same. This character knows that the life of an artist is filled with hardships and obstacles along the way. How does this character feel about this? What does their art mean to them? Would they rather give up now when they're just getting started or chase their dreams regardless of how tough the road may seem?

073 - 076

What is the most terrifying of all: killing another human being, finding their dead body, or... having to look into the eyes of a widow and tell them that their husband is no more? What does it take to become a coroner? Is it courage, a sense of duty, or a ruthless desire for a paycheck?

073

The Coroner

Write about a character who happens to be a coroner. How did this character end up in this odd profession? Was it a trick of fate, or did they always want to become one? What goes through the head of this character in the moments before they talk to a widow? Explore the thoughts of a character whose job is to deliver bad news. And, above all, how do they deal with the stress? Do they make a joke of death or... drink themselves numb?

074

Private Ryan Didn't Make It

Write about a character who happens to be a coroner and has been tasked to deliver some horrible news to an elderly woman. The last of all of her children was found dead. How does this character face the reality of telling a mother that she has outlived all of her children? What goes through this character's head as they knock on the woman's door?

075
Oscar Winning Performance

Write about a character who happens to be a coroner. While doing their job, this character finds that the person they're giving the bad news to doesn't seem fazed... at all. For a moment, this character is certain that they see a glint of joy in the person's eyes. How does this character react to this? After a professional career of seeing widows cry, how does this character feel about someone who seems *happy* about the death of their loved ones? What could possibly be the reason behind this?

076
Last Set of Bad News

Write about a character who happens to be a coroner, and they have just one day left until their retirement. They have one last house to visit and one last set of bad news to deliver. How does this character feel about their last day on the job? After so many years of delivering bad news, do they regret anything? Do they feel like they've done a great service to the world or simply been cleaning up the mess left behind by Death?

077 - 080

What's harder: to become an inspiration or to stay inspirational? What happens when someone who was an example to millions of people, someone who represented human excellence, falls from grace? Were they never good to begin with – or were the expectations of the world too great?

077

The Fallen Paragon

Write about a character who was once a source of inspiration but is now nothing but an old joke. Fallen from grace and the public eye, this character is nothing but a shadow of their former self. What exactly happened in the past; how did they 'fall' from grace? Who stayed with them, and who left them? After so many years, does this character look back to those days with a smile on their face or tears in their eyes? Did they really enjoy being a 'paragon'?

078

Why Do We Fall?

Write about a character who was once a source of inspiration but is now nothing but an old joke. Although this character may have lost their public image and their wealth, they have not lost their will to fight and continue inspiring people. Where do they draw courage from? Why do they choose to go on when everyone turned their backs to them? Who are they doing all of this for: themselves or someone very dear to them?

079
Is That You, Lucifer?

Write about a character who was once a source of inspiration, except this character did not 'fall' from grace; they were dammed by the public eye. What were they blamed for, and why did everyone believe it? Could it be that this character truly deserved it? If this character had a chance to speak to the world one last time, what would they say?

080
Not an Icon but a Man

Write about a character who once found inspiration in a person, except said person has now fallen from grace. What did this person mean to the character? What is this character's first thought when they come face-to-face with the person they used to look up to? Do they see remnants of the inspiration this person was? What does this character have to say to this person? Is that a tear of joy in their eyes... or sadness?

081 - 084

Do all authors dream of fame and fortune? What happens when they achieve that? Their books have been turned into a successful series of movies, they've written episodes of their favorite TV Shows; they have not only become an inspiration for other writers, but also a cultural icon. And yet... is it possible that they're still not happy?

081

The Best-Selling Author

Write about a character who happens to be a best-selling author. Their life may seem easy and luxurious from the outside-in, but could it be there's more to it? Explore the life of a best-selling author who has achieved critical success, yet they still stay up at night. What do they think about in the dead of night? Do they believe they've earned their success? Is there anything they regret about the past? And, most importantly, what is the *one* story they've never had the guts to write?

082

Meet Richard Bachman

Write about a character who happens to be a best-selling author. Over the years, this character started writing under a pen name so that they could publish their more controversial books. Whose idea was this? How does this character feel about hiding their real identity to protect their 'brand?' What does this character do when their pen name suddenly enters the public eye? How far is this character willing to go to keep their alter-ego secret?

083
My Reflection

Write about a character who happens to be a best-selling author. As this character is out and about, they're approached by an aspiring author who barrages them with questions. How does this character react to this? Does this happen often? What does this character see when they look into the eyes of that aspiring author? Is it just another lazy writer looking for a quick-way to get rich… or could it be it's a reflection of who this character once was? What is the *one* greatest piece of advice this character has for that aspiring author?

084
Pretty Penny

Write about a character who happens to be a best-selling author. Over the years, this character has written books that have never been printed; out of all of them, there's a book that is different than the rest of them. This character promised themselves that they would never, ever, publish this book. Why did they make this promise? What's so special about this book that it has to be hidden? What is keeping this character from simply burning this book to make sure no one ever reads it?

085 - 088

We live in a cruel world. People who've done no wrong are stepped on by those with more desire than heart. But what of the people who have been wronged? What of the silent members of history who were nothing but stepping stones for the tyrants and, at times, the heroes?

085
The Whisperer

Write about a character who was wronged in the past by cruel people. They've been broken so many times that they no longer speak up. This character only talks in whispers… but are their minds this quiet? Is there fire left in their hearts, or is their courage nothing but embers? Does this character remember those who wronged them? What would this character do if they found themselves alone in a room with the people who were cruel to them in the past? Would this finally be the time to raise their voice?

086
The Betrayer Will Become The Betrayed

Write about a character who was wronged in the past by cruel people, except that this character has been waiting for their chance to strike back— and the time is nigh! What is their plan for revenge? What goes through their mind in the seconds leading up to striking back at their foes? Do they question their motives? Do they have any second-thoughts about repeating the cycle?

087

Forgiveness is the Attribute of the Strong

Write about a character who was wronged in the past by cruel people, except that when given the option to seek retribution this character chooses to not do so. Why do they hold back when the world has been cruel to them and offered no apologies? What does this character do when they realize one of the people who wronged them is about to strike again? Is there a limit to this character's patience and forgiveness?

088

It Was Nothing Personal

Write about a character who has wronged many people during their life. Why did they choose to trample on others as a way to rise to the top? How do they rationalize it? If they could turn back time, would they change things? And, worst of all, how does this character react when they come face-to-face with someone they wronged many times in the past?

089 - 092

Is there such thing as a 'normal' person? In a world with so many places and cultures, can that really exist? What would their background be like? Would they even consider themselves 'normal?' There has to be something out of the norm in their history – right? Or is it possible that their 'normality' is within itself abnormal?

089
The 'Normal' Person

Write about a character who considers themselves 'normal.' Why does this character want to be like this: has it been by choice, or has society simply programmed them to be this way? Do they find safety in being part of the crowd, or do they feel they're trapped inside of a cage? How does this character react when they meet someone who is not like them? Explore their thoughts as they come face-to-face with someone who shows no interest in anything 'normal.'

090
The Times, They Are A-Changin'

Write about a character who considers themselves 'normal,' except that the world around them is changing— and with it, the standards of 'normality.' How does this character feel about this change? What do they do when they realize that their entire sense of identity is in danger? Is this character willing to change with the times so that they remain 'normal?' What does being 'normal' mean to them?

091
Our Only Salvation... Is This Guy

Write about a character who considers themselves 'normal,' and it just so happens that this character is the key to humanity's survival. What can this character do that no one else can? Why did this character consider themselves 'normal' all of their life? How do they feel about the fact that, regardless of what they've done, their life has become extraordinary? If they had a chance... would they give this responsibility to someone else?

092
Don't Be So Vanilla

Write about a character who stumbles upon a person who claims to be absolutely 'normal.' How does this character react to meeting this person? How do they feel about the concept of being 'normal?' Do they consider themselves anything close to that? What does this character really see in the person before them: someone who is ironically strange, or a sad person trying to fit into society's expectations? Is this character willing to tell this person what they think— to their face?

093 - 096

As humans, we want to believe that we'll live forever, and the prospect of our own mortality terrifies us. There are some among us, though, who witness the thin balance between life and death on a daily basis. They are our modern-day healers. The Surgeon can be both the harbinger of doom and the angel of second-chances.

093

The Surgeon

Write about a character who happens to be a surgeon. How did this character end up in this profession: was it by choice or need? How does this character feel about the fact that lives depend on them? How would this character react if they realized they've lost their first patient? Who do they blame for that loss? And, worst of all, what does this character do when they're approached by a relative of the dead patient?

094

It's Not the Same, I Know You

Write about a character who happens to be a surgeon, except that this character finds themselves having to operate on one of their closest friends. Did this happen by chance, or did the friend choose this character to be their surgeon? How does this character feel about this? Are they willing to let someone else do the operation, or do they believe this is something only they can do? And, when the time to operate comes, do they feel their hands tremble for the first time in years?

095

Doctor House, You Have to Save My Wife

Write about a character who happens to be a surgeon, and they are tasked with operating on a pregnant woman. Except something goes wrong during the operation. The clock is ticking, and this character needs to make a choice. To save the mother would damn the child, and to save the child would damn the mother. There's no way to save both. What does this character do?

096

Doctor Repa

Write about a character who was a master-surgeon, except that a horrible accident has left them without an arm. This character is told that they cannot ever operate ever again, and with that, never save another life. How does this character react to the news? Do they feel they've lost their purpose in life? What good is a surgeon who can't operate? Could it be there's hope for the future or only despair?

097 - 100

Is amnesia just another literary trope? How would it really be to lose one's memory — to be damned to experience everything again as though it was new? Could it be that, maybe, amnesia is the perfect escape from the nightmares of our past, complete freedom at the cost of everything we know...

097
The Blank Slate

Write about a character who wakes up one morning and do not recognize anything or anybody around them. What does this 'new' world look like from their point of view? Has this character truly forgotten everything or only some things? Does this character have any idea how they lost their memory? And, worst of all, what does this character do when they come face-to-face with someone who claims to have been their spouse?

098
Finding Who?

Write about a character who is suffering from amnesia, except that, regardless of their condition, they're certain that someone needs them. This character strongly believes that without their aid, that person will suffer a horrible death. What's the first thing that this character does? Do they have any idea where this person may be? And, worst of all, is this person... real? Or could it be that their mind is playing tricks on them?

099
Total Recall

Write about a character who is suffering from amnesia, except that only a few parts of their memory seem damaged. They remember their work and their daily life— but none of the people involved in it. How does this character deal with meeting everyone for the "second time"? Is there anything strange with these people? Could it be that… maybe this character is not suffering from amnesia at all?

100
Sunshine of the Spotless… Something?

Write about a character who is suffering from amnesia, except that they remember everything and everyone in their life… except *one* person. What is the relationship between this character and this forgotten person? Is it possible there's a reason why all of the memories regarding this person have disappeared? What happens when this character comes face-to-face with this person and feels that they used to be more than just acquaintances? Is their mind playing tricks on them… or could it be that it's trying to protect them?

101 - 200

Story Seeds that start with
LOCATIONS

"If you are lucky enough to have lived in Paris as a young man, then wherever you go for the rest of your life, it stays with you."

Ernest Hemingway

101 - 104

What leads to a quiet bedroom? Is it the lack of communication between two people who once loved each other? The bedroom is fit for its purpose — but the TV is off, and there is neither laughter nor fighting. When was the last time this bedroom was filled with their sounds?

101
The Quiet Bedroom

Write about a quiet bedroom. What does this place look like? Why is this place so quiet? Is there anyone in the room or is it empty? A bedroom should be a place for resting, but why is this room not being used like that— or could it be it has another, hidden purpose? If this room could talk, what would it say?

102
The Place We Used to Call Home

Write about a quiet bedroom, except it has been abandoned for decades. Although no one lives there anymore, people still come in every year or so to clean and make sure the room, and the rest of the house are not falling apart. Who is doing this? Why would someone keep a place in good repair but not live in it?

103
A Line Dividing the Bed Sheets

Write about two characters who find themselves in a bedroom. They're sitting on separate sides of the bed, and, although they have a thousand things to say to each other, they are both quiet. What is the relationship between these characters? Did something happen long ago or in recent memory? What is keeping them from voicing their thoughts? Are they quiet because they're afraid… or could it be that the silence is exactly what they've been looking for?

104
Deathly Quiet and No Witnesses

Write about a character who finds themselves in a bedroom… except that they're lying on the floor, dying a slow death. What happened to this character? Explore their final thoughts. Do they think anyone is going to find their body, or is no one going to care? What is the very last thing that goes through this character's mind: do they regret anything, or do they feel they had it coming?

105 - 108

What happens when the teacher has to leave to take a call? For a few minutes, there will be no authority in the classroom. The students could do as they please – but does everyone want anarchy?

105
The Loud Classroom

Write about a classroom and the students in it. The teacher is gone, the clock is ticking, and everyone wants to take advantage of this opportunity. Who is planning to prank the teacher? Who wants to play with their friends? Who wants the teacher to return as soon as possible so that order is restored? And, above all, who is going to start the chaos?

106
Duck and Cover

Write about a loud classroom, except that the source of the noise is not the students. Something is happening outside; what is it? What can the students see from the classroom windows? Is there a reason for them to worry? Could it be the source of this noise has something to do with the call that sent the teacher away? What would the students do if they realized the teacher was *not* coming back?

107
The Chance to Strike

Write about a classroom and the students in it. Their teacher is gone for the moment, and a handful of students take this as their chance to gang up on one of their fellow students. What reason do they have for doing this? Are they just bullies or... enacting their revenge? What do the other students do? Do they step in and try to stop the fight, or do they watch in silence? And, worst of all, what is their teacher going to find when they walk back into the classroom?

108
Down With Homework!

Write about a classroom and the students in it. Their teacher is gone for the moment, and a few students take this as a chance to stir chaos — property is damaged, people are hurt, and the police is alerted. What happens once the dust settles? Who is going to pay for the damages? Are the chaotic students going to face charges, or will 'blind' justice punish all the students in the classroom? After all, it happened when the teacher wasn't around — who is to say all the students weren't in on it?

109 - 112

In the farthest end of the park, where no one ever ventures, there's a lonely bench. A place like that should be run-down, but the bench is in pristine condition, and the path leading to it is clean. Who would sit in that bench in the loneliest place in the park?

109
The Lonely Bench

Write about a bench that is always empty, regardless of the time of day. What does this park look like: is it welcoming to visitors, or does it scare them away? Is there a history behind this park? Who is the person keeping this bench, and the path leading to it, clean? Why would this person bother cleaning that bench, especially when no one ever sits there?

110
The Place Where We Met

Write about a bench that is always empty... except there was a time when it wasn't so lonely. A young couple used to sit on that bench, but they haven't been seen in years. What happened to them? Could it be there's a connection between that young couple and the strange person who keeps that bench in pristine condition?

111
Urban Legend?

Write about a bench that is always empty… except that, over time, it has become the subject of an urban legend. They say that whoever sits on that bench will suffer a horrible death within twenty-four hours. Is there truth behind this legend, or is it just a story to scare children? What would happen if… a teenager was dared to sit on that bench?

112
The Bench at the End

Write about a bench that always seems to be empty… except for certain times of day, when a strange person can be seen there. This individual is known for having a weird ability. What can this person do that has earned them such an odd reputation? What would happen if… a young person approached this stranger, asking for their help?

113 - 116

Everyone is always going somewhere or doing something. We live in a busy world. No one has time to sit down and chat – but, what if they had to? What if they were stuck in a place where all they had to do was sit around and wait?

113
The Broken Elevator

Write about a broken elevator and the unfortunate characters who happen to be stuck inside of it. Explore the thoughts of these characters as they realize they're not going anywhere for a long while. Do these characters find company in each other, or do they fear that one of them may not be what they claim to be? Worst of all, how do their emotions change after one hour? What about after ten?

114
The Elevator Club

Write about a broken elevator and the unfortunate characters who happen to be stuck inside of it. As the hours pass these characters realize they have something in common: an experience they thought was unique to them. What do they share in common? Does this realization bring them closer together or solidify their reasons not to trust each other?

115

You Don't Understand, We're All Gonna Die

Write about a broken elevator and the unfortunate characters who happen to be stuck inside of it. As one of the characters realizes they're not going anywhere, they begin to panic and attempt to find a way out. How do the other characters react to this? Is there really a reason to be afraid? And, worst of all, could it be that time is *not* on their side?

116

Down the Rabbit's Elevator

Write about an elevator that keeps going down, regardless of the attempts to stop it. Where is the elevator going? What do the characters see when the doors open? Are they back in the world they're familiar with or... somewhere *wonderful*?

117 - 120

Romance can happen in a million places, but it seems to linger in coffee shops. Between the aroma of fresh coffee and the chatter of young voices, there appears to be the soft whispers of two hearts becoming one… Except when they don't.

117
The Coffee Shop

Write about a coffee shop, and the two characters who spot each other across the room. These characters notice each other— and they feel the primal need to flee. But they don't. Explore the thoughts of these characters. Why do they choose to stand their ground when their first reaction was to run away? Do these characters have a history? They can't stand still for too long, who makes the first move?

118
A Different Game of Chess

Write about a coffee shop, and the two characters who spot each other across the room. These characters notice each other— and do *nothing* but sip their coffee and glare. What happened between the two of them? Is either of them willing to go and talk to the other? Or could it be they're both planning to drink their coffee in silence and walk away?

119
One Week

Write about a coffee shop, and the two characters sitting across from each other at the same table. Neither of them talks or makes eye-contact. What happened between them? Is one of them at fault— or could it be that both of them feel guilty for what happened? Which of these two characters will be the first to speak?

120
My First Love

Write about a coffee shop and the two characters who're sitting down and chatting. These characters used to be in a relationship, and after years of anonymity after the breakup, they decided to sit down and 'catch up.' Why did they breakup in the first place? How has each character changed over time? Do they feel that they made the right choice with ending the relationship— or could it be that the 'spark' is still there?

121 - 124

Why would someone break into a church in the dead of night? Would they do it out of personal gain... or out of a desire to experience the church in a way that is not possible during daytime?

121
The Empty Church

Write about a character who breaks into a church. What does the church mean to them? Is it still a symbol of safety and faith— or has it fallen from grace? What does this character seek to gain by breaking into this church? Is this character looking for something they can sell for profit, or... could it be this character is looking for salvation?

122
The Priest Who Lived

Write about a character who breaks into a church, except that this character used to be priest of that church before it was closed. What happened back in those days? What has become of this church? Why has it taken so long for this character to return? And why is breaking into this building the only way for this former priest to be at peace?

123
The Clergy Has Enough

Write about a character who breaks into a church, seeking to steal as much as they can. Is this character doing this out of greed, need, or could it be they're trying to send a message? What is the *one* thing that this character is not willing to steal and why? Do they have a personal reason— or could it be they're afraid of divine retribution?

124
A Different God

Write about a character who breaks into a church and discovers that all of the iconography is of a large obsidian monster. What is the meaning behind this place? What reason did this character have for breaking in to *this* building? Did they enter to find proof of that strange monster or to sit down and pray?

125 - 128

Some may claim to not believe, and others may claim that they've seen strange visions in their dreams. Regardless, they're all the same: they entered the fortuneteller's chamber seeking knowledge. They're more curious than afraid. Unfortunately, they are not opening not a present, but Pandora's box.

125
The Fortuneteller's Chamber

Write about a character who goes to see a fortuneteller. What is the first thing that this character thinks when they find themselves surrounded by incense and candles? Do they truly believe that the fortuneteller can help them? What is this character looking for? Do they dare look into the crystal ball or touch the tarot cards? Does this character find what they were looking for— or could it be that they've had the answer inside of them all along?

126
The Falling Tower

Write about a character who goes to see a fortuneteller. During the tarot reading, the fortuneteller reveals that the character is about to face great strife and danger— their entire life is about to collapse on itself. How does this character take the news? Do they believe the words of the fortuneteller or... could it be this is what they feared all along?

127
The Sun

Write about a character who goes to see a fortuneteller. During the tarot reading, the fortuneteller reveals that the character is going to experience a golden age— they will succeed at their goals and grow closer to achieving their life-long dreams. The future is looking bright... but is this what the character wanted to hear? Can they truly believe that things are finally going to go their way? Could it be that it's easier to believe a horrible fortune than a good one?

128
The Stars are Not in Position!

Write about a fortuneteller as they attempt to read a customer's fortune— but they are unable to. What is this fortuneteller's first reaction? Do they offer an explanation, or do they quickly try another method? How does their customer react? What is wrong with this customer's future? Are the stars disrupted— or could it be that said customer doesn't *have* a future?

129 - 132

There's a fine line between exploring a large mansion thinking that one may find something and actually discovering a secret. How would this explorer react when they press a seemingly invisible switch and, just like that, a wall opens up. Have they found what they were looking for, or have they gained nothing but more questions?

129
The Secret Room

Write about a character who finds a secret room inside of a mansion. What reason does this character have for wandering around this place? Are they looking for treasure or closure? How did they find this secret room? What do they find within— have they stumbled upon a family secret or something truly extraordinary?

130
The Dark Descent

Write about a character who finds a secret passage leading underground. There's no way to know how far the passage goes or where it leads. What is the first thing this character thinks when they see the odd passage? Did they find it by mistake or had they been searching for a long time? Is this character willing to go down the passage? What means the most to them: to live another day or to find out the truth?

131

A Secret Named Sophie

Write about a character who finds a secret room inside of a mansion— except that this room contains a person. How does this character react to the discovery? Do they recognize the stranger? Could it be they haven't seen each other in years, or is the stranger inside that room not human?

132

Mystery of the Past, or the Future?

Write about a character who finds a secret room inside of a mansion— except that they don't recognize the technology within. What is the first thing this character notices about this strange technology? Have they stumbled upon relics of old... or days that have yet to come?

133 - 136

A basement may be nothing more than a place to store things... but what if it kept a horrible secret? What is that smell? Is it coppery like pennies? Or disgusting like rotten eggs? What is the source of that smell, and why is it only coming from the basement?

133

The Dank Basement

Write about a character exploring a basement that smells... *odd*. Do they know what they're going to find or are they seeking answers? Explore the senses of this character as they explore the basement. Does this character see weird shapes beyond the darkness, or is their imagination playing tricks on them? What truly lies in that basement— and what's the source of that *horrid* smell?

134

Did I Do That?

Write about a character exploring a basement, and during the process, they discover a corpse. What is this character's first reaction to seeing this? Do they recognize this corpse? And, worst of all, do they tremble at the sight of that dead body... or do they feel like it's not the first time they've seen it?

135
Is That You, Hugo?

Write about a character exploring a basement, and in the process, find a person chained to the floor. Does the character exploring the basement know who this person is? Is there history between them? Why would that person be chained to the floor of the basement? Could it be… this is their punishment?

136
A Whisper in the Darkness

Write about a character exploring a basement, except that upon entering this place the character feels an overwhelming urge to leave. What happened to the odd smell that drove this character to explore it in the first place? Is this the first time this character has tried to explore the basement? What truly lies at the bottom of that place, and is this character brave enough to find out?

137 - 140

Theme parks are a bastion for those seeking excitement, thrills, and laughter. But once night falls, the place takes on a different air. The house of mirrors reflects faces one does not recognize, and the laughter of clowns can almost be heard in the darkness. Who would be brave enough, or foolish enough, to venture into such a place?

137
The Theme Park at Night
Write about a character who finds themselves in a theme park at night. How did this character end up here? Did they seek to find something lost, or were they dared into it? Explore their thoughts, fears, and courage as they explore a place that would be fun in the daytime, but not so much at night. Wait— what's that sound? Is that... laughter? Did the merry-go-around just turn on?

138
One Last Time
Write about a character who finds themselves in a theme park at night. This character has a personal reason for being there. What does the theme park mean to them? Is this the place where they first fell in love, or are they the previous owner of this theme park? What drives this character to break in at the dead of night and sit on the benches overlooking the Ferris wheel?

139
Lakeside Amusement Park

Write about a character who finds themselves in an *abandoned* theme park at night. What reasons does this character have for doing this? Are they alone? How does this character react when they hear distant laughter and the sounds of rusted attractions bursting into motion? Is that a smile on their face, or are they terrified?

140
Another Urban Legend

Write about a character who finds themselves in a theme park at night. Except this theme park is the subject of an urban legend. They say that at midnight, the phantoms of the children who died in an accident wander freely, turning on the rides and laughing in their eternal childhood... but it's all a story, right? The character entering this theme park keeps telling themselves that they are not afraid, even as their sweaty hands begin to tremble.

141 - 144

In the back of the library, there's an odd place. The books have dusty spines, and they don't appear to be organized in any particular order. What sort of librarian would leave such a mess?

141
The Unlabeled Section

Write about a character who stumbles upon a section of the library without any labels. What does this place look like? Is it a disorganized mess, or does it appear mundane? How did this character end up in the unlabeled section? What sort of books does this character find here? Is there something *odd* about those leather-bound tomes?

142
Years That Will Never Come Back

Write about a character who stumbles upon a section of the library without any labels, but soon discovers that the books are old yearbooks. What do these books mean to this character? Is this what they were looking for, or trying to get away from? Is this character brave enough to open the yearbook and gaze at who they used to be?

143
The Book That Spoke

Write about a character who stumbles upon a section of the library without any labels, and as they begin to inspect the shelves, they hear whispers coming from somewhere. How does this character react to this? Is their imagination playing tricks on them— or is one of the books talking to them? What is the voice saying? And, worst of all, is this character willing to do what it says?

144
Curiosity Intensifies

Write about a character who stumbles upon a section of the library without any labels, and as they begin to inspect the shelves, the librarian kicks this character out. Is this enough to deter this character from doing that ever again? How do they feel about the librarian's explanation or were they not given one? What does this character plan to do? Are they more curious about those books than they are afraid of the librarian?

145 - 148

They say that our workplace says more about us than our work. Could this be true? Does this apply to a writer and their desk?

145

The Writer's Desk

Write about a writer's desk. What does this place say about its owner? Is it a reflection of the way the writer makes their stories, or a reflection of their mind as a whole? And, most importantly, where is the owner of this desk? Why are they not at their desk writing?

146

Drifting, Slowly Drifting

Write about an abandoned writer's desk. Something happened to the writer, and it's been a very long time since they last sat down and put words to paper. What happened to the owner of this desk? How has this place changed in their absence? If this desk could talk, what would it say?

147

The Call I'd Been Waiting For

Write about a writer as they pace around the room with phone in hand. On the other side of the line is the person who is going to make their dreams a reality. What is the person on the phone promising? Is this truly what the writer wants? And, most importantly, what does the writer see when they look at their desk? Do they see the workstation of an artisan or a prison?

148

A Story Forgotten

Write about an abandoned manuscript locked in the deepest drawer of the writer's desk. Explore the point of view of this item. Why is this manuscript locked away? What sort of story is written on its pages? For how long has it been gathering dust? And why won't the writer finish this story?

149 - 152

The city can be a cruel place, and yet, it can be beautiful. At night, from the rooftop of a building, the countless lights of the city create a second starry sky. In moments like those, people can fall in love, find much needed courage, or come to terms with the past.

149
The Rooftop

Write about a character sitting on the rooftop of a building, looking up at the sky. What is going through this character's mind? Why did they escape to that place? Did they find what they're looking for? What do they think about the city as they leave the rooftop? Is it a place of beauty or cruelty?

150
I Knew I Would Find You Here

Write about a person sitting on the rooftop of a building, looking up at the sky— except this character is not alone. A person from their past has found them. How does the character react to this person? Were they expecting company? What did this character really want: to be left alone or to have someone find them?

151
Last Night in the City

Write about a character sitting on the rooftop of a building, looking up at the sky— one last time. What is this character's history with the city? Are they leaving because they've found a better place to be… or is it because the city defeated them? What is that in their eyes? Are they crying because it's over or because it never began?

152
I Don't Recognize You Anymore

Write about a character sitting on the rooftop of a building, looking up at the sky— except this character is very old. They grew up in the city, and after so many decades, they realize the place they grew up in doesn't exist anymore. What runs through this person's mind as they look at the city skyline? Do they long for the days of their youth, or do they wish they had been born in a different era?

153 - 156

What does it take to take a person's breath away? Is it merely natural beauty – or could it also be terror? The harsh truth is that both the wonders of the world and the battlefields of war can take our breath away.

153

The Breathtaking View

Write about a breathtaking view. Explore not only its appearance but also its history. Was it always this breathtaking, or did something make it so? What other feelings does it inspire? Is this view a monument to a grand civilization, a natural wonder, or the aftermath of a horrible event? If this place could offer one piece of advice to future generations, what would it be?

154

What Happened, My Dear?

Write about a character as they look at a place that only they consider to be breathtaking. What does place mean to this character? How is this view 'breathtaking?' What would this character do if they encountered another person who felt the exact same way?

155

It Wasn't Always Like This

Write about a place that used to be breathtaking, but it's not anymore. Explore the history, and the future, of this place. What made it so breathtaking years before? What changed? And, is there a chance that this place may once again be what it used to, or has its fate been set in stone?

156

I Have No Words Left to Speak

Write about a character as they look at a breathtaking view. They're so moved by it that they're unable to speak. What does this place mean to this character? Why have they suddenly lost their voice? Explore this moment without dialogue or thoughts, only actions.

157 - 160

There is really no safe haven out in nature. A cave may protect one from the rain and the cold, but there's no way to know if one is walking straight into the mouth of danger... But what if that was your only option?

157
The Cave

Write about a character who finds themselves inside of a cave. How did this character end up here? Were they seeking shelter from the weather, or are they fleeing from danger? How do they battle the darkness inside this cave; do they brace against the walls blindly or do they have a light source to guide their way? Is this cave more than what it seems? Does it lead to a strange place— or is it home to a creature that is better left undisturbed?

158
Watch Your Step, Goldilocks

Write about a character who finds themselves inside of a cave— except this character realizes, a moment too late, that they've walked into a group of sleeping bears. What does this character do? Is it safe to flee, or is there no other way than through? How does this character react when they see one of the bears slowly open its eyes?

159
The Truth is in There!

Write about a private investigator who finds themselves inside of a cave. This character is certain that the clue they need to solve their case lies somewhere inside that cave. Why is this character willing to put themselves in danger— is it all for a paycheck, or do they have personal reasons? What does the case mean to them?

160
A Different Purgatory

Write about a character who finds themselves inside of a cave. After hours of walking deeper and deeper, the cave doesn't appear to lead anywhere… it just keeps going and going. What does this person do when they begin to wonder if the cave is endless? Can they even see the way they came through? Could it be this character doesn't even remember how they got there in the first place?

161 - 164

161

The Cold Campfire

Write about a character who stumbles upon an empty camp. How do they react? Were they looking for company, or were they trying to get away from someone? Is this character looking for supplies? Are they willing to take them from that camp at the risk of angering the owners? Or... could it be that camp has been abandoned for a long time?

162

Where Are You Guys? This is Not Funny

Write about a character as they return to their camp after collecting wood for the fire— except their friends are gone. What is this character's first reaction to finding the empty camp? Where have their friends gone? Are there any clues as to what happened to them? Should this person be worried?

163
A Mystery Left in Pieces

Write about a private investigator who stumbles upon an empty camp. This character looks at the world differently than most people; to them, everything is a piece of evidence. Describe their mental process as they start examining the camp. Do the clues lead effortlessly to the answer, or is there more to that camp than meets the eye?

164
The World Has Gone to Hell

Write about a character who stumbles upon an empty camp. Except this character is a scavenger, and they're delighted to find the camp empty. Write from their perspective as they start filling up their bags with supplies. Has the world really gone crazy, or is this character the only one willing to benefit from the misfortune of others? What would this character do if the owners of that camp suddenly showed up?

165 - 168

Is the human mind programed to flinch at the sound of thunder? Could one ever find beauty in such a thing — or is it nothing more than nature's reminder that she will not be tamed?

165

The Thunderstorm

Explore thunder not as a decoration— but a trigger. Write about a character who has a history with the sound of thunder. What does that sound remind them of? Is it a fond memory or one they would like to forget? What would this character do if they found themselves in the center of a thunderstorm? Why are the trembling — is it because of fear or excitement?

166

Baby's First Thunder

Write about a child who hears thunder for the first time. How do they react? How does this child rationalize this monstrous sound? Is there anyone around to explain what is going on, or is this child all alone?

167

It Reminds Me of Fourth of July

Write about a character who loves thunderstorms, to the extreme that they would travel great distances to witness them. What drives this character to do this? What history do they have with thunderstorms? And, what would this character do if the 'storm of the century' was coming their way— would they risk their lives just to witness it?

168

The Furious Sea

Write about a character who is on a boat and trying to make their way to shore— except that there's a terrible storm, and they're not sure if they can make it through. Is this character all alone on the boat, or do they have company with them? Is this character afraid of dying at sea? What would they do if they saw a wave, big enough to swallow their boat whole, coming towards them?

169 - 172

Stranded... all alone. There's no way to escape, and no shelter. There may be sources of food and water deeper in the island... but are you brave enough to enter?

169

The Deserted Island

Write about a character who finds themselves stranded on a deserted island. What is the first thing they do when they realize that their fate is entirely in their hands? Explore the mind of this character. What do they do? Do they rush into the jungle, or are they paralyzed by fear? For the first time in their entire life, they have no one else to depend on, no one else to get them out of their troubles. But are they really all alone in that island?

170

No One is (Ever) Alone

Write about a character who finds themselves stranded in a deserted island. At night, this character can hear a strange chanting coming from somewhere in the jungle. How does this character react to this? Are they excited to find company... or are they worried that the other people may not be friendly? Worst of all, what happens when the chanting grows louder and louder?

171

I Wish I Could Tweet About it

Write about a character who finds themselves stranded in a deserted island. This character used to live in a big city, and they were very dependent on technology. Can they survive without their cellphone or computer? What does this character do when they realize just how dependent they were on their technology?

172

Peace at Last

Write about a character who finds themselves stranded in a deserted island— except that they feel no rush to go back to civilization. Why is this character so happy to be in such a place? Is this really what they've been looking for all of their life?

173 - 176

How strong is the perception of innocence? What would it take for a children's room to become something… terrifying?

173

The Toy Room

Write about a character who finds themselves in a child's toy room. What reason does this character have to going into this place? Do they have a history with this room? What are they looking for? Is there anything *odd* about this toy room? And, worst of all, where is the child?

174

Leave, and Never Come Back

Write about a character who finds themselves in a child's toy room— except that this place has been closed off for decades. Why would this character open it up? What do they seek to find? And, most importantly, why was the room closed off in the first place?

175

Fear is in the Eye of the Beholder

Write about a character who finds themselves in a child's toy room. Although this place looks mundane, the character is terrified by what they find. What is there to be afraid of in that toy room? How do the people around this character react to their fear? Could there really be anything odd about that room— or could it be that this character sees something no one else can?

176

They're Just Like He Left Them

Write about a character who finds themselves in a child's toy room— except that this place does not inspire terror, but sadness. What did this place meant to the character? Why do they feel like crying whenever they look at that room? And, worst of all, what happened to the child who used to play in that toy room?

177 - 180

What does a courtroom mean to someone facing trial? What does it mean to the victim of a terrible crime? Is there any honor to be found – or is it merely just a place to avenge the lost and make examples out of people? Justice should be blind and fair... but what happens when it's not?

177
The Courtroom

Write about a courtroom and the moments leading to the verdict. A courtroom should be a place to right wrongs, but what happens when the people there are corrupt? What goes through the mind of someone who faces great charges for a crime they didn't commit? Or, even worse, are being punished for doing the 'right' thing?

178
The Jury Trembled

Write about a courtroom and the moments leading to the verdict, except the defendant is someone hated by the public and has been accused of dozens of terrible crimes. Who is this person? Are they really as bad as the media claims? And, worst of all, what happens when they're found not guilty? What do they have to say to the world, and how does the media react?

179
Silent Certainty

Write about a courtroom and the moments leading to the verdict, except the defendant hardly spoke at all during the trial. What is going on inside their head? Why do they find no need to defend themselves? Are they regretting their actions... or are they confident that they won't be facing any punishment?

180
No Justice Left in the World

Write about a courtroom and the moments leading to the verdict, except the persecutor is lying. They are using false evidence, and they've paid the right people to make sure the defendant is found guilty. And they will succeed. Why trick the system? Is this persecutor willing to do anything for a paycheck, or do they have a personal vendetta against the defendant?

181 - 184

How much money is 'too much' money? Where is the line between wealth and decadence? Can one person be too rich? Or is this a thirst that cannot be appeased?

181

The Penthouse

Write about the home of a character who is 'too rich.' What does this place look like? What does this home say about the character who lives there? Could it be that so much wealth has corrupted the character living there, robbing them of their humanity? What would happen if the character who owned this home was as humble, kind, and generous as a saint? Could such a thing even be possible?

182

The Luckiest Person Alive

Write about the home of a character who is 'too rich,' except that said character has not earned a single dollar in their life. Every part of their enormous wealth has come by sheer luck: given, found, and won. What does money mean to this character? What would they do if they simply lost it all in the blink of an eye?

183
Mine, Mine, Mine

Write about the home of a character who is 'too rich,' except said character is very protective of their wealth — to the extreme that they would never let anyone else see it, for fear that they would steal it. What does wealth mean to this character? Why would they rather hoard it than make use of it? And, worst of all, what would happen if a thief robbed them while they weren't looking?

184
The Temple of the Gods?

Write about a place of ridiculous wealth, and the commoner who finds themselves there. How did this character stumble upon this luxurious home? How do they react to seeing so much wealth in one place? And, worst of all, would this character dare and steal from this place — or has the sight of it changed their mind about wealth?

185 - 188

Growing up, we are often told to learn from the mistakes of others... but we are stubborn creatures. How often does a person hear a word of warning, only to say: "I'll be fine, that won't happen to me."

185

The Warning Sign

Write about a stubborn character and the strange warning sign they stumble upon in the middle of nowhere. What does the sign read? Is it a matter of life and death? And, worst of all, has the warning come too late?

186

You've Got to be Kidding Me

Write about a stubborn character and the strange warning sign they stumble upon in the middle of nowhere— except there's not one but *two* signs. To make matters worse, each sign is warning about a different threat. How does the character react to this? Could it be one of the signs is lying? Or, worst of all, what if both signs were nothing but a trick?

187

Yet Another Urban Legend

Write about a stubborn character and the strange warning sign they stumble upon in the middle of nowhere. There's an urban legend that speaks of a warning sign in the middle of the desert, and those who read it will know when and how they're going to die. Could this be true? What sort of person would travel so far to find out? And… could it be they're too late?

188

This is Ironic

Write about a stubborn character and the strange warning sign they stumble upon in the middle of nowhere— except this sign is in another language. How does this character react to this? Is there a way to find out what the sign says? Is there enough time?

189 - 192

There are a few places in the city a person should never go to unless they're looking for trouble. Out of all of them, dark alleys are the worst. Only a fool would walk into a place like that willingly, because their curiosity will be rewarded with nothing but a knife in the back. But — what if this was the best out of two bad options?

189
The Dark Alley

Write about a character who finds themselves in a dark alley, not by mistake, but by choice. What brought them to this place? Were they looking for something or trying to *get away* from someone? What does this character do when they realize they're not alone, and worse— there is no way out?

190
Venus Flytrap

Write about a character who finds themselves in a dark alley, not by mistake, but by choice. Except this character is not alone; someone is following them into the alley. And yet, this character doesn't appear to be worried at all. What are they planning to do? Is this character looking for a little privacy with their 'friend,' or is one of them walking into a trap?

191
Wrong End of the Law

Write about a character who finds themselves in a dark alley— except this character is a criminal trying to evade the police. A sensible person wouldn't have run into an alley, especially one that looks like a dead-end. Why is this character going there? Are they out of options, or do they know something about that alley that no one else does?

192
Anniversary of that Day

Write about a character who finds themselves in a dark alley, not by mistake, but by choice. This character is carrying with them a bouquet of roses, which they proceed to put on the floor at the end of the alley. What does this place mean to them? What is the story behind the sadness in their eyes? And, most importantly, why are they not afraid of that dark alley?

193 - 196

Like trees sprout from seeds, there has to be a place from which fear sprouts. What would push a person to be afraid of a house? What would drive an adult to stay away from a building? Is it fear of the people within — or fear of what the house means?

193

The House

Write about a character who is too afraid to set foot in a house. What does this place look like; is it anything to be afraid of? What happened in the past? What planted the *seed* of fear in this character's heart? Is there anything they can do to overcome this fear, or has the seed taken root?

194

They Say the Place is Haunted

Write about a character who is too afraid to set foot in a house— except that this place is the subject of many urban legends. What would drive this character to enter the house? Are they trying to impress someone, or are they trying to convince themselves that the legends are not true? Do they find what they're looking for... or do they find *more*?

195

Oh, It's You Again

Write about a character who is too afraid to set foot in a house. In the past, this character has tried to overcome their fears and has failed each time. But they're willing to try again. Why can't this person rest until they rid themselves of that fear? What drives them? Is it courage or guilt? What would they do if they were unable to overcome this fear?

196

I Heard About Mom

Write about a character who is too afraid to set foot in a house because that was the place they grew up in. They ran away decades prior, promising themselves that they would never set foot in that place— but something happened. Why did they leave in the first place? And, most importantly, why would they return after so many years?

197 - 200

Along the road of life, we travel to many places searching for happiness. Is life then nothing more than a quest to find the right place? The right tree that will forever bear the perfect fruit? Is such a thing even possible?

197

The Place (I Was Meant to Be)

Write about a character who believes they've finally found a place to call 'home.' For how long have they been looking? Did they sacrifice anything along the way? What does this place provide that they can't get anywhere else? And, most importantly, is this really the place they're meant to be?

198

The End of a Journey

Write about a character who believes they've finally found a place to call 'home.' Explore the mind of this character as they reflect on their life, and consider the trials they had to face to end up in that place. Do they think it was all worth it? If they could, would they change anything about their past?

199

Not What I Expected

Write about a character who believes they've finally found a place to call 'home.' Except this character quickly realizes that this place is not as great as they originally thought. What happened? Did the place change… or did this character change? What do they have left to do? Will they simply pack up their bags and start searching again?

200

Not a Place, but a Person

Write about a character who believes they've finally found the person they're meant to be with, someone who provides them with everything they had been searching for. What's so special about this person, and do they feel the same way?

201 - 300

Story Seeds that start with
OBJECTS

"It has long been an axiom of mine that the little things are infinitely the most important."

Arthur Conan Doyle

201 - 204

What's the meaning behind the wedding band? To many, it's a symbol of everlasting love… but does it retain that meaning when it's found laying on the ground?

201
The Wedding Ring

Write about a character who finds a wedding ring. What is this character's reaction to finding this item? What does this item look like? Is it a bargain ring or a diamond-studded beauty? What does this character do— are they willing to pocket this ring? After all, no one is looking for it, right?

202
It's a Sign!

Write about a character who finds a wedding ring, and realizes that this is their chance to propose to the love of their life. Do they go through with this? How do they think their 'love' will react? Is this character planning to tell their 'love' where the found the ring?

203

You Can Keep It

Write about a character who finds a wedding ring, only to stumble upon the owner within seconds. To the character's surprise the owner doesn't want the ring back. How does the character react to this? Describe the owner's body language. What does the owner's motions say that they're not willing to speak out loud?

204

The Ring of the Lords

Write from the perspective of a ring laying on the ground. How did it end up lost? Who did it belong to, and why is it no longer with them? Was this ring lost or... abandoned?

205 - 208

There's a story behind every picture. Some may be innocent, funny, sad, or all of the above. A photo is a piece of the past, forever frozen in the moment it was taken. The question is: has the story behind the photo survived time – or has it been forgotten?

205
The Family Photograph

Write about a character who finds a family photograph. Who is this character? Do they recognize the people in the photograph? How has time affected this item? Is this picture a reminder of happier times... or something darker?

206
I'm So Sorry

Write about a character who finds a family photograph— except this character made a terrible mistake in their youth. How did that event impact the people in the photograph? Has time changed any of that? Does seeing this photograph give this character closure, or has it only succeeded at opening old wounds?

207
Evidence
Write about a character who finds a family photograph in a crime scene. This item is one of the few clear piece of evidence they're able to find— but what does it mean? What happened in that crime scene, and what does it have to do with the people in the photograph? Is this the breakthrough the character was looking for, or has the plot only thickened?

208
You Should've Apologized Sooner
Write from the perspective of a family photograph as someone picks it up. Does this photograph know the person who found it? What does this item think of the events that happened when it was taken? If it could talk, what would it say?

209 - 212

Stuffed animals are more than just cloth and fluff. Ask a child who has ever been afraid at night, and they will speak of their companions – their fellow fighters – who fend off the monsters that lurked in the shadows. Warriors in bright colors with button eyes.

209
The Stuffed Animal

Write about a child and their favorite stuffed animal. What does this item look like? Where did it come from? Was it purchased from a shop or made by a loving hand? Is this stuffed animal more than just a toy to this child?

210
Teddy: Monster Slayer

Write about a child who is terrified of the darkness, to the extreme that they're certain there are monsters in their house— and that the only one who can fend them off is their favorite stuffed animal. Where are the child's parents? And, most importantly, is it all in the child's head, or could it be that there is something strange going on in that house?

211

I Was Already Old When I Met You

Write from the perspective of a stuffed animal as it's being gifted to a child. What is this item's history? Is that child their first owner? How old is this stuffed animal, and what has it experienced in those years?

212

Hello Again, Peter

Write from the perspective of an adult who finds their old stuffed animal. Do they have fond memories of this item? When was the last time they saw each other? How have they changed over the years?

213 - 216

What goes through the mind of a child playing with little soldiers? Are they really just toys? What about in times of war? What do toy soldiers mean to a child whose parents are off fighting in the front lines?

213

The Toy Soldiers

Write about a child whose parents are fighting in the ongoing war. What happens when this child looks at their favorite toy soldiers? Are they still something to play with, or have they taken upon a new meaning? What about the war? What does this child know about it? Do they think their parents are coming back, from hearing so many stories of victories, or is their family's silence making them worry?

214

Only War

Write about a child who lives in a world where war is a common happening. How do adults explain this to the child? Which has lost all meaning: war or human life? How has the child been impacted by this?

215
How Did They Die?

Write about a child whose parents died fighting in the ongoing war. Who is left to take care of this child? Are they willing to tell this child what happened... or would they rather lie? How does this change the way the child looks at their toy soldiers?

216
All For Nothing

Write about a parent who returns from the war, whole and safe, only to realize that in their absence their only child passed away. What happened to the child? Is there anyone to blame? How does this affect the parent? What do they do now that they've had to outlive their children?

217 - 220

Ragged clothing, oddly shaped eyes, dirty face. Who would care to pick up such an ugly toy? It was thrown in the trash for a reason, right? But... what about its origin? What about the person who made it?

217
The Ugly Doll

Write about a character who finds an ugly doll in the trash. What does this item look like? What exactly makes it 'ugly?' How did this doll end up here? What does this character do when they find it? And, most importantly, what do they see when they look into the eyes of that doll?

218
The Failed Toymaker

Write about a character who used to be a toymaker. What does this ugly doll mean to them? Did they make it, or does it remind them of their once-beloved profession? Most importantly, what do they do with this doll? Do they throw it back in the trash like their dreams or... dare to try again?

219

Human Effigy

Write about a character who finds a doll of themselves in the trash. Is the similarity uncanny, or are certain features exaggerated? What does this character do with this doll? Is it simply just a prank, or is there something *odd* about this doll?

220

I Thought You Loved Me

Write from the point of view of an ugly doll found inside a trash container. What is their side of the story? How did they end up there? Were they always 'ugly?' Who put them in the trash? If they could get payback for everything that happened to them, would they?

221 - 224

There is not a single blank page in this notebook. A lot of work, and a lot of love, must've gone into the words and the drawings… why would anyone abandon something so precious?

221
The Notebook

Write about a character who finds an abandoned notebook. What does this item look like? What exactly is written and drawn in it? What is this character's first reaction to what they find? And, above all, do the contents of the notebook touch their heart?

222
I Was Once Young Too

Write about an elderly character who finds an abandoned notebook. As they read the contents of the notebook, they remember the days of their youth. Did they once have a notebook similar to it? What happened when they were younger? Do they look back on those days with a smile on their face or a frown? And, most importantly, how do they feel about the author of the notebook?

223
Last Goodbye

Write about a character who is looking for their missing friend. As they search the friend's house, they find a notebook. Is this the first time this character has seen this notebook? What is written inside? Does it provide any clues as to where their friend has gone or... is it just a long goodbye letter?

224
I'm Pretty Sure That's Not English

Write about a character who finds an abandoned notebook. As they start looking at the pages, they notice that everything on it is written in a strange language they've never seen. How do they react to this writing? What do they do when they see the sketch of what appears to be a monstrous creature? Does this character take the writing and sketches seriously, or do they think they're merely part of a prank? What happens, though, when a strange person cloaked in black arrives to pick up the notebook?

225 - 228

The handwriting is careful, almost beautiful, for something written on a napkin. To another person, they would be nothing more than lines on paper, but to you... they are seven digits of glory.

225
The Phone Number

Write about a character who wakes up after a night of drinking and finds a phone number written on a napkin. What happened the night before? Do they remember the person who wrote the number? This character can't help to smile when they look at the seven digits— but why? What about this makes them so happy? Do they really long for that person's company, or do they plan to use that number for something else?

226
We Knew You'd Call

Write about a character who wakes up and finds a phone number written on a napkin inside one of their pockets... except they didn't go out drinking the previous night. Has this character ever been to a bar? What were they doing the previous night? Is this character the target of a prank, or did they forget what happened? And, above all, does this character have the courage to dial up the number on the napkin?

227
Wrong Number

Write about a character who gets a call from a stranger who claims they met at a bar the previous night. Unfortunately, this is something that happens to this character often. Explore their mind as they get yet another call. Who is doing this to them? Why would someone willingly give out this character's number? Is there anything this character can do about it?

228
Greatest Night of Your Life, Maybe?

Write about a character who wakes up after a night of drinking and, upon finding a phone number in a napkin, starts trying to piece together what happened the previous night. They only remember three things with clarity: (1) They went there with a friend but said friend is no longer with them; (2) they met someone who they found to be incredibly attractive, either mentally or physically, but they don't seem to remember anything else about said person; and (3) the place they find themselves in is completely unknown to them. Write about this character as they try to piece together what happened. Do they call the number on the napkin, do they look for their friend, or would they rather find out where they are? Most importantly, though— what exactly happened the previous night?

229 - 232

The surface of the cards is smooth, worn by the nervous fingers and the shattered dreams of strangers hoping to win big... in a different place, it would be a tragedy, but such is the life of a deck of cards in a casino. Success or failure. Wealth or poverty. They're all part of the game.

229
The Deck of Cards

Write about a character who is addicted to gambling, to the extreme that they've started idolizing their deck of cards. Each suit means something different to them. Hearts. Spades. Clubs. Diamonds. They're all part of their life philosophy and, to the surprise of the people around them, this character carries themselves pretty well. How do they justify gambling? And, most importantly, how is it that this addiction has not weakened them but actually made them stronger?

230
Lucky As Hell

Write about a character who made a deal with the devil. In exchange for their soul, they've gained the power to win at games of chance with just a snap of their fingers. What does this character do with this power? What happens when money is no longer an issue? And, worst of all, what do they do when they realize that their ability may affect more than games of chance?

231

King of Diamonds, Dethroned

Write about a character going through a terrible life crisis that demands a large sum of money— which they are unable to generate. Quickly running out of choices, this character decides to gamble it all. What sort of life crisis would push them to do this? Why is gambling their last resort? And, worst of all, would they turn around if they knew, in advance, that the casino is going to rob them blind?

232

It Was Fun While it Lasted

Write about a character who is addicted to gambling, but doesn't seem to be at all interested in making money. Whenever they win, they simply hand the money over to family, friends, or even strangers. Is this character charitable in nature, or do they find no value in money? What do their friends and family think of them? Do they take advantage of this character? What would happen to this character if one day they simply grew tired of gambling? Worst of all, what would their 'friends' and family have to say about this change?

233 - 236

What does it mean to carry a cane? Is it a sign of weakness – or proof that a person is driven to move on? A cane may represent a hundred different things, but all of them resonate with a similar meaning:

'I will not stand still.'

233

The Cane

Write about a character who needs a cane to walk. Explore life from their point of view. Have they always needed a cane to walk, or is this the result of a recent change? How does this character feel about the cane? What does it mean to them? Do they carry this cane with pride or shame? And, worst of all, what would happen if their cane... disappeared?

234

Latest Fashion

Write about a character who uses a cane even though they don't truly need it. What does the cane mean to them? Is it an accessory, or is there a darker purpose to it? Worst of all, though, what does this character do when they stumble upon a person who actually needs a cane to walk? Who is the first to talk, and what do they have to say?

235
A Different Torch

Write about a young character who needs a cane to walk and thus are gifted the cane of one of their late grandparents. What is the history of this cane? Is this the first time it has been passed down? How does this young character feel about the present? Do they find shame in such an antiquated item... or does it inspire them to go on, much like it inspired their ancestors?

236
Lean On Me

Write from the perspective of a walking cane. How does this item see the world? Who is their current owner? Is it someone young or old? If this cane could talk to their owner, what would it tell them? How does it feel to truly live a selfless life, giving support and aid to others without ever asking for anything in return?

Your phone does everything. You can send emails. Stay up to date with the world. Watch videos. Browse the internet. And a thousand things more. Your phone is your link to the world... why, then, would a person willingly dispose of something so useful?

237
Goodbye, Smartphone

Write about a character as they dispose of their smartphone. What goes through their mind as they toss the phone out the window, or crush it with a hammer? Why would they do such a thing? Was it all just an act of defiance against the system— or against a single person? Most importantly, though, what are they going to do now that they're finally 'free' from the network?

238
Goodbye, Evidence

Write about a character who committed a terrible crime and has been systematically removing everyone who knew about what they had done. At last, the final witness of their crime is in their grasp: a smartphone. Who was the original owner of this item, and what happened to them? What sort of crime did this person commit? What were their reasons behind it? And, worst of all, what do they do when they realize that the smartphone in their hands is a fake?

Goodbye, Love

Write about a character who lost their spouse in a terrible accident. Over the many months, they have gotten rid of most of their late-spouse's possessions… all except their smartphone. This character knows that if they turn the phone on they will find pictures and messages of their beloved— the same way they left them the day they died. This is the last item this mourning character needs to get rid of… but are they willing to do so? Do they simply dispose of the phone, or do they dare turn it on and look at their beloved one last time? What would their reaction be if they found more than they bargained for?

Goodbye, Matrix

Write about a character living in a society where people are dependent on their smartphones for *everything*. This character, unlike everyone around them, desires to free themselves from that bind. Is this character truly willing to let go of all the advantages of that technology? What sort of struggles do they face? What does it mean to live outside of the internet, in a world where everyone is jacked-in?

241 - 244

What is the meaning behind a white dress? Is it meant to represent a blank page, a new beginning, or is it meant to imply the purity of the wearer? Would this meaning change, at all, if the dress was covered in dust?

241
The Wedding Dress

Write about a character who finds a wedding dress in their attic. What is this character's relation to the dress? Has time been kind to this item, or what was once white and 'pure' is now looking moldy and gray? And, most importantly, how could something as precious as that end up in an attic?

242
No Glass Slippers to be Found

Write about a character who finds a wedding dress in their attic, except said dress appears to be untouched by time— and dust. The dress looks and feels like something out of a fairy tale, but… could it be? Explore the thoughts of this character as they examine this strange item. And, most importantly, are they willing to find out what happens when someone wears the dress?

243
We Meet Again, Old Friend

Write about an elderly character as they look at their old wedding dress. What does this dress mean to them, so many decades after they last wore it? How do they look back on those days? If they could, what one piece of advice would they give to their younger self?

244
A Bargain

Write about a character as they find a pristine wedding dress at a yard sale. The price tag says that the dress is on sale for one dollar— but can it be? Explore the interaction between the character and the person selling the dress. What do their expressions say that they would never speak to one another? And, if the dress could talk, what would it say?

245 - 248

Underneath the bed, there's a chest. Inside the chest, there's a shoebox. Inside the shoebox, there's a little book... but who would go through such a length to hide that little thing. What could possibly be hidden inside the pages of that diary?

245
The Secret Diary

Write about a character as they find a diary in their room. Was this character looking for this item— or did they stumble upon it? What do they find written inside that diary? And, most importantly, is this character the author of the diary... or a stranger?

246
Is This Who I Was?

Write about a character who suffers from amnesia and is trying to piece together their past. What goes through their mind as they read the pages of their old diary? Do they relate to the author— or do they feel like they're two entirely different people? For how long can this character reach for the past before realizing that, maybe, they're better off starting anew?

247
What You Don't See On TV

Write about a detective as they inspect a diary found at a crime scene. Explore their thoughts as they examine the diary, page by page, in hopes of finding out a clue as to what happened. Why is this item so important? And, most importantly, was this diary owned by the victim... or the criminal?

248
Super Duper Level Secret

Write from the perspective of a secret diary as it is being read by a complete stranger. Who is this person? What business do they have trying to read this diary? Worst of all, though, how does the diary feel about the fact that they know more than its pages reveal? Does it find pride in holding secrets that will never be known or long to share the truth of what really happened in the past?

249 - 252

The envelope is yellow. The post-stamp is faded. The paper smells moldy and acidic. Why would the postman deliver something so... old? What sort of message is trapped inside that envelope, and how long did it take for it to finally arrive?

249

The Untimely Letter

Write about a character as they find an old letter in their mailbox. Who is the letter addressed to? Does it have a return address? Is this character willing to read the letter within or... could it be that they recognize that letter? Is it a piece of their past, once again returning to haunt them?

250

Return to Sender

Write about a character who continuously keeps mailing the same letter to themselves. What reason could they have for doing something like that? For how long have they been doing that? What exactly is inside that letter? And, worst of all, what happens when their postman finally approaches them and asks about it?

251

Dear Future Self

Write about a character who finds an old letter in their mailbox, except they recognize the envelope. It's a letter they wrote to themselves a long time ago. Does this character remember what they wrote in the letter, or has it been so long that they've forgotten? Do they dare open the letter and find out just how much they've changed over the years... or would they rather leave the past behind?

252

I Don't Even Own a Mailbox

Write about a character who is always traveling, moving from place to place and never settling anywhere. Explore their reaction as the postman delivers them a letter. How does this character react? What does the letter mean to them? Worst of all, the contents of the letter pushes them to return to the place they fled from decades prior. What does the letter read, and who wrote it?

253 - 256

What's a gemstone but a pretty rock? Is there a true value behind jewelry — or is the perception of value what lures people to make great expenses? Diamonds, gold, and silver. What would be of them if the world considered them mundane?

253
The Underpriced Gemstone

Write about a character who makes jewelry, except that they severely underprice their stock. What is the meaning behind this? How do people react to seeing jewelry that should cost thousands of dollars going for mere hundreds? Do people take advantage of this — or do they second-guess the source of this character's jewelry? And, most importantly, why would a person who creates something so precious sell it so cheap?

254
Diamonds: Dime-A-Dozen

Write about a character who is about to sell an enormous amount of diamonds for practically nothing. How did they find the diamonds? Who is the person willing to buy them without hesitation? Is the character tricking the buyer — or are they simply naive? Above all, who benefits the most from the sale: the buyer or the character who gets rid of the diamonds?

255
This Will Go Great With My Wedding Dress

Write about a character who, while shopping for jewelry, finds a person who sells used wedding rings. How does this character react to the 'stock?' Are they willing to buy a used wedding ring for a very low price — or do their values stop them? What does a wedding ring mean to them? And, worst of all, what happens when they recognize one the rings in the 'stock?'

256
The Raven's Gem

Write about a character who, while shopping for jewelry, stumbles upon a salesman who claims their rings have 'magical properties.' What do these rings look like? How does this character react to the salesman's claims? Could it be that the rings are truly magical — or is it merely a trick to sell jewelry? There is only one way to find out, right?

257 - 260

Who gains the most from a gravestone? Is it just for the living so that they can remember their loved ones? Who can, with certainty, ever say that the dead really want to be remembered?

257

The Gravestone

Write about a character as they witness the burial of a friend. What was their relationship like? Is this character looking for closure, or are they simply giving their final goodbye? Most importantly, though, what was the last thing that this character said to their friend— and why is it the only thing they can think of?

258

The Unmarked Gravestone

Write about a character as they witness the burial of a 'friend,' except the gravestone is... blank. Explore the thoughts of this character, as they watch their friend's remains be forever bound to a nameless grave. Was this the friend's wish, or could it be that this character wants no one to remember their so-called 'friend?'

259
New Neighbors

Write from the perspective of a ghost as a new person is being buried on the adjacent grave. What do they think about their new 'neighbor?' How old is this ghost? How do they feel about being bound to the gravestone? And, above all, what does the new 'ghost-on-the-block' have to say?

260
Second Chances

Write about a character who experiences their own burial, like a phantom hovering over the grave. Who came to their funeral? What did they have to say? What does this character regret the most? And, worst of all, what would happen if they were to suddenly wake up — alive — and realized they had a second chance to live?

261 - 264

What is the purpose of a weapon in times of peace? Is it merely a sign of wars long past? What does it mean when this 'sign' of victories, courage, and honor begins to… rust?

261
The Tarnished Sword

Write about a character who owns a very old sword. Has time been kind to this item? How did this character find this sword? Did they simply stumble upon this weapon… or has it been in their family for generations? What does the sword mean to this character, and what would they do when they hear the news that war is looming in the horizon?

262
It's Dangerous to Go Alone

Write about a young character as they're given a sword to defend their family. Who was the previous owner of this weapon? Why is it that this young character is the only one who can defend their family? What does this character think of this 'present?' What does the sword mean to them? What goes through their mind as they realize that with the sword they could easily… kill anyone?

263
Bloody Hands

Write about a character as they look at their family sword. This character enjoys wealth and fame, though their family took those by force. What does this character think when they look at that sword, the same that cut the throats of anyone who stood against their family? Does this character regret being born into that bloodline— or have they grown too used to the feeling of blood on their hands?

264
The Price of Peace

Write from the perspective of a sword as it is being sold in an auction. What is the history of this weapon? How does this item view the things it did in the past? Does it consider itself a killer or merely a weapon used by men with cold hearts? Worst of all, what does this item think when it's sold for an insignificant amount of money?

265 - 268

How did cloth and color become the face of a nation? How can a white banner bring relief to soldiers, and a black flag atop a mast strike fear in the hearts of sailors? A flag is just cloth and dye, right?

265
The Flag

Write about a character as they see a flag in the distance. Are they lost at sea or fighting on the front lines? Explore what a flag means to this character and to the people around them. Is it just a symbol, or does it mean much more? Worst of all, what does this character do when they recognize the flag is drawing closer and closer?

266
The Forgotten Nation

Write about a soldier as they witness an army in the distance that bears a strange flag. This soldier has never seen anything like it— and neither has their superiors. What goes through their mind as the enormous army advances closer to them? What does this soldier do? Do they believe this army is a friend or foe? And what do they do when they remember a legend they heard long, long ago?

267

White Flag

Write about a soldier as they wave the white flag of surrender. What goes through their mind as they become the sign of their army's defeat? For how long did they endure? How many losses did they suffer? And, above all, how does this soldier think history is going to remember them... if they will be remembered at all?

268

Red and Black

Write from the perspective of a group of young characters as they make plans to overtake their government. Why have they set themselves on such a dangerous mission? Are they chasing fame, fortune, or revenge? Describe their flag. How does it represent their movement? If said flag could utter a word of warning to these young characters, what would it be?

269 - 272

What is the greatest boon to pass down to the next generation? Wealth and fame could make the life of one's children easier... but what about values? How long does it take for gold to simply tarnish and lose all worth?

269

The Family Treasure

Write about a character as they're handed their family's treasure. What does this item look like? What's the history behind it? And, above all, what does this character think of their heirloom? Does this item excite them for the future, or do they realize that their time has come to bear the burden of their family sins?

270

Not Found, but Stolen

Write about a character as they steal what will later become their 'family treasure.' What does this item look like? Is this character attaching a belief to this item, or is the value behind it evident to all who see it? And, worst of all, will the descendants of this character ever find out that their 'family treasure' was stolen?

271
What's in the Box?

Write about a character as they're handed a wooden box, said to contain their family treasure. Has this character been looking forward to this day? Were there any trials they had to overcome in order to finally get that box in their hands? However, what is their reaction as they realize that the wooden box is... empty?

272
Dark Origins

Write from the point of view of a family treasure. What is this item's history? How did it end up in the possession of this family? Was there a time when this item served a... different purpose? If this item could talk, what could it say to the character it's being passed down to?

273 - 276

What will the future think of us and the things we did in our time? The world changes so fast and so drastically – who is to say that the world will look the same a hundred years from now? Who is to say that we will be remembered… at all?

273
The Time Capsule

Write about a character as they are building a time capsule, a small container filled with items from their era, to be buried in the ground so that it can be found by the people of the future. What are they putting inside the capsule? What need does this character have for leaving something behind? What is driving them to do this? Do they seek to be remembered, or are they afraid that their people will be… forgotten?

274
Hello Again, Me

Write about a character as they dig up their old time capsule. What do they find inside? How much time has passed? Explore the thoughts of this character as they start examining the contents within. Has time changed this character, or has it only affected the items in the capsule?

275

Time as a Witness

Write about a character as they bury a time capsule, not out of a desire to be remembered, but rather to be forgotten. What horrible truth did this character hide inside that capsule? And, above all, did they do it to protect themselves or to protect the world?

276

Time Capsule, Reversed

Write about a character who finds a time capsule buried in their backyard. How did they end up discovering the capsule? Explore the thoughts of this character as they examine the items within. Has time been kind to these items? And, above all, what is this character's reaction as they find a letter addressed to them?

277 - 280

It's done. There are no more cries in the dark. The air is stained with a metallic scent. Death is not meant to be pretty or quiet – but the knife is, if anything, the quietest of all killers.

277

The Bloody Knife

Write about a character as they find themselves holding a bloody knife. At their feet there's the mutilated body of someone dear to them. What is their first reaction to the sight of the knife and the body on the floor? Do they remember what happened? And, worst of all, what do they do when they hear police sirens off in the distance?

278

The Bloody Knife, Reversed

Write about a character as they find themselves lying on the floor, bleeding. Standing above them, they see a person dear to them… who is holding a bloody knife in one hand. Explore the thoughts of this character as they lose consciousness. What goes through their mind in their last moments? Do they have questions left unanswered, or were they expecting to meet this fate?

279

Double Bloody Knife

Write about two characters as they find themselves in a desolate place. Without warning, they pull out weapons and start swinging at each other. Why are they doing this? Are they surprised that they were not the only one with murder on their minds... or were they expecting a duel to the death? In a battle between two blood-thirsty people, can there be a clear winner?

280

The Angel's Knife

Write from the perspective of a knife with a thirst for blood. What is the history of this strange weapon? Does it whisper dark desires into the minds of its wielder, or does it seek those who also thirst for blood? What does this item do when it finds itself in the hands of someone too kind and too pure-hearted to ever hurt another person?

281 - 284

All families have secrets; sins of the past, lies told through white teeth, goodbyes punctuated with a knife on the back. What matters is not 'what' really happened but making sure that the skeleton stays in the closet, forever.

281
The Skeleton

Write about a character with a terrible family secret, something so horrifying that they're certain they would lose everything if the truth was found out. How do they go about making sure the truth stays hidden? How has a life of secrecy changed this character? And, worst of all, what happens when someone they trust starts asking too many questions?

282
My Parent's Bones

Write about a character whose parents were killed by a wealthy and influential family. Many years later, this character returns to their hometown to settle the score. What is their plan? How do they intend to avenge their parent's death? Are they willing to repeat the same injustices that happened to them? And, worst of all, what happens when they discover that their parents weren't killed in cold blood— but in an act of self-defense?

283

Not a Skeleton, but a Child

Write about a young character who is locked in the attic by their family. What reason is there to hide this character? Who is to blame: the family or the character? How does this young character rationalize being locked away from the world? And, above all, do they have dreams of someday leaving that attic— or are they afraid of repeating the past?

284

The Crimson Skeleton

Write from the perspective of the remains of someone who was murdered and is now being kept as a trophy by the killer. Explore the thoughts of a pile of bones. Who was this person before being killed? Did they know the murderer? Reflecting upon its past, what do these bones have to say about the day they died? And, above all, why is it that they are not at all bitter about what happened?

285 - 288

What's the true value behind gold? What does money mean to a person starving and dying of cold? What would happen to the richest person in the world if suddenly their gold was worth nothing and they were hungry and freezing?

285
The Golden Coins

Write about a wealthy character who is lost in the wilderness. What's the first thing they notice about the place they find themselves in? For how long will their designer clothes and jewelry keep them warm? Are they willing to let go of their possessions so that they can travel faster? Describe in detail what it feels for this wealthy character to feel hunger and cold for the first time in their lives. And, above all, *who* do they blame for all their problems?

286
Fort Knox

Write about a character who finds a boxful of golden bars in their basement. Describe their reaction. Who do they run to tell first? Or... would they rather keep it a secret from those who would take the golden bars for themselves? Is this character at all worried about the source of these items? What is their reaction when they realize that there is no 'legal' way to make money off the bars?

287
Currency Depreciation

Write about a character in a world where coins mean nothing. Survival is key, and the value behind gold and gemstones is nonexistent. Explore their thoughts as they sell their treasures for a mere loaf of bread and hundreds of golden coins for a blanket. What happened to this world, and what does this character think of it? Do they feel that they're being wronged, or are they jealous of those who have food to eat and a fire to keep them warm?

288
Where is George Now?

Write from the perspective of a dollar bill as it passes from hand to hand over time. What does this item think of the people it comes in contact with? How does it feel about being worth so little? If this item could offer a piece of advice to its latest owner, what would it say?

289 - 292

What is the need to leave flowers at a grave? The dead have no need for trinkets or presents. Could it be that they are not for those who passed but those who remain? Is that really an act of love or an act of selfishness?

289
The Lonely Rose

Write about a character as they leave a single rose at a grave. What was their relationship with the person who died? Is this their first time visiting the grave, or is this something they do every once in a while? Explore the reasons behind this character's need to see the grave. And, above all, what does this character say to the grave that they would've never told the person when they were alive?

290
Two Roses

Write about a character as they leave a single rose at a grave... and then they notice someone else joins them. This second person also leaves a single rose. What is this character's reaction to seeing the second person? Is this the first time they've met? Does this character see their grief mirrored in the other person— or are they suffering from a different sadness?

291
Magic Trick

Write about a character as they leave a single rose at a grave... except that the grave has their name on it. Who is this person, and how were they successful at faking their own death? What need was there to escape the world they lived in? And, above all, who was the person buried in that grave?

292
Lies That Transcend Time

Write from the perspective of a gravestone as someone leaves a single rose. The person standing before the gravestone believes it to be the final resting place of someone dear to them... except they're wrong. Explore the thoughts of the gravestone as, year after year, the same person shows up and grieves the loss of someone who was not buried in that grave. And, if this gravestone could talk— would it reveal the truth to the person or let them mourn an empty grave?

293 - 296

Leather bound, stained with patches of dark red and smelling of ashes and copper. Who could've made such a book? And… what reason did they have for hiding the words written within?

293

The Strange Tome

Write about a character who finds a strange tome in the depths of their basement. They're not sure why… but they're afraid of it. How do they rationalize being terrified of a book? Is this truly the first time they've come in contact with this item? What do they do when simply looking at the tome drives chills down their spine? And, worst of all, are they at all curious about what could be written within?

294

Your Story

Write about a character who finds a strange tome in the depths of their basement. As they start reading the pages, they realize that the book has written on it the story of their lives. Everything is written in extensive detail. What is this character's reaction to this? What does this character do with the tome? Are they willing to skip over to the last page and find out how their story ends?

295

The Next Nostradamus

Write about a character who witnesses strange visions of the future and writes them down in their notebook. When did this character start experiencing these visions? Why did they decide to write them down? And why would anyone with the ability to look into the future not attempt to profit from it? What horrible truth of the future does this character know that they would rather keep hidden from the world?

296

The Necronomi-Something

Write from the perspective of a strange leather-bound tome. What is its history? Is this tome just odd-looking, or is there something darker to it? Who is the latest owner of this tome? How did they find it? And, worst of all, what plans does this tome have for their latest 'owner?'

297 - 300

What happens when experiments go wrong? Who is to blame? Are humans curious beings by nature or should they know better than to play 'God'?

297

The Vial

Write about a scientist as they realize they've created something beyond their wildest dreams. Explore the thoughts of the scientist as they look at the little vial in their hands. What does this mean to them? Did they arrive at this result by chance, or were they working on this for years? What lies inside that little vial? Is it a chance to renew the world, a poison to burn it to the ground... or could it be something even worse?

298

The Cure

Write about a scientist suffering from a terrible disease. After years of testing, they're finally able to create a cure... but they're not the only ones who need it. Explore the mind of a scientist who holds the fate of countless people in their hands. Taking the cure would mean their survival— but what would the world think of a savior who put their lives first before everyone else?

299
The Virus

Write about a scientist who was tasked with creating a chemical weapon for the government and has finally completed the *virus*. What drove this scientist to take the job and see it through? How do they feel about their creation being used to kill thousands upon thousands of people? Who do they blame for the weapon: the government that demanded it, the enemy's unbreakable will, or… themselves?

300
The Experiment

Write from the point of view of a lab rat as it is the subject of experiments. What does the rat think of the scientists? What effect have the experiments had on the rat's body and mind? And, worst of all, what happens when the experiment goes wrong? Does the lab rat suffer an untimely death… or does it become something unlike the world has ever seen?

301 - 400

Story Seeds that start with
SITUATIONS

"It is by suffering that human beings become angels."

Victor Hugo

301 - 304

A home should be a place where one feels safe and welcome… but what if there is none of that? What if one's parents argue and fight too much? To the hearts without warmth, the cold road feels like salvation.

301
Running Away From Home

Write about a young character who runs away from their home. What are their reasons for leaving? What does this character take with them, and what do they leave behind? What goes through their mind as they walk the cold and dark road? Is that sadness in their eyes or tears of joy?

302
Also a Bon Jovi Song

Write about a character who, as they're driving home, see a young runaway walking on the side of the road. What does this character think of this runaway? Was there ever a time when they felt like the only solution was leaving it all behind? And, above all, is this character willing to pull over and give the runaway a hand?

303
Cold but Not Alone

Write about a young character who runs away from their home, except that they're not alone. They're not the only person running away that night. Write about this young character's interactions with the second runaway. What do they share in common, and what is different? Do they know each other? And, above all, did they run away for the same reasons?

304
Lost and Found

Write about a parent as they finally find their runaway child, except it has been several decades. How have parent and child changed in these years? Who is the first to speak— and what do they have to say? Are the first words threats, screams, or muffled sobbing?

305 - 308

In relationships, there's no such thing as a trial period or a return policy. The only way to really test if the person you're interested in is worth your time is to... take them out on a date. Like playing the lottery, though, not all numbers are winners.

305
The First Date

Write about two characters out on their first date. Have they known each other for a long time? Where did they meet? Do they have feelings for each other, or are they testing waters? And, worst of all, why is neither of them talking? Are they not having fun, or are they too nervous?

306
Wrong Table

Write about two characters out on a blind date. Whose idea was this, and how do either party feel about this? What happens within the first minutes? Do they connect, or do they share awkward silences? And, worst of all, what happens when they realize that one of them is sitting at the wrong table?

307
Second First Date

Write about two characters out on a date, except that this is not the first time they've tried for a relationship. What happened in the past? What is these character's history, and what prevented them from going 'steady' in the past? And, above all, why are they so willing to try again?

308
Lottery Winner?

Write about two characters out on a date. Within seconds, they realize the other person is perfect for them. Explore the minds of both characters as they discover that the person in front of them is everything they've ever wanted and more. But... can it be true? Is there such thing as a 'perfect' match? What are these characters hiding from each other— and is that reason enough to make them part ways?

309 - 312

There's a certain flare to the first move in a game of chess – but what about the second move? Is there really value behind a great opening with a lazy follow-up? What happens when a great first date leads into a not-so-great second date?

309
The Second Date

Write about two characters being out on their second date. How did their first date go? Do they have different opinions on how it went? Where are they going for their second date? Explore the very first moments of the night – does it have a promising start, or can both characters feel that the relationship has run its course?

310
More Chess Analogies

Write about two characters being out on their second date, except one of them really doesn't want to be there at all. Explore their game of 'relationship chess' as one character tries to have a great second date and the other is trying to sabotage it. Does either party catch on to what is going on? And, most importantly, who is the winner of that match?

311
Finishing the Promise

Write about two characters being out on a date, except that this is their second attempt at finishing a date that was cut short. What interrupted their date? Why did they feel a need to give the date another try? How has time affected each character? And, worst of all, what happens when they realize the person before them is not the same they went out on that date that was interrupted so many years before?

312
Even Hotter Than Before

Write about a character who is out on their second date, except that their date doesn't quite look like they did before. Their date, who appeared to be one gender on the first time they met, now looks like an entirely different gender. Explore the thoughts of the first character as they have trouble recognizing their date. What happens then? Is this character willing to drop their date on basis of looks alone, or is the appearance of their companion not a problem to them? What does this character do, though, when they realize that the people around them are looking at them funny?

313 - 316

Being in a relationship is like trying to disarm a bomb. A person can watch a lot of movies and think it looks easy, but when they actually try, they find that there's more to disarming a bomb than just cutting wires and praying. The biggest difference is that when a relationship blows on your face, you don't get the benefit of dying and not having to deal with the fallout.

313
The Third Date

Write about two characters being out on their third date. How has their experience gone so far? Are there still big questions that need to be answered? Is this date just a formality? What would happen if one of the characters didn't want to go through with the relationship? It's been three dates. Are they going to attempt disarming the bomb— or are they wearing a flak jacket and are bracing for the explosion?

314
Even More Bomb Analogies

Write about two characters being out on their third date, except that they hate each other with a burning *passion*. Two dates were more than enough to show them that they're not compatible. Why did they decide to go for a third? What happened in the two previous dates; why were they such *duds*? And, above all, could it be they're looking to end things with a *bang*?

315
Sorry, Sorry, Sorry

Write about two characters being out on their third date, except that they know the relationship isn't going to work out, but they don't want to tell the other person. Are they both extremely shy or just afraid of conflict? Do they both realize what is going on? And, above all, what are their final words as they decide to part ways?

316
Two Broken Toys

Write about two characters being out on their third date. They're not a perfect match, but they enjoy each other's company. What is keeping them from being 'perfect' matches? Are they willing to change for each other, or would they rather call it quits and start looking somewhere else? Explore the very last moments of the date, as both characters realize the have to make a choice and time is not on their side.

317 - 320

Fingers touching, heart racing, eyes closed, and then — like magic — lips come into contact. Two warmths become one, and for an instant, the world seems to come to a stop. Is it really magic, or is it nothing more than chemical reactions?

317
The First Kiss

Write about two characters as they share in their first kiss. Where is this moment taking place? How old are these characters? Explore their thoughts as their kiss comes to an end. What do they really think? Is this a moment they will cherish the rest of their lives... or something they would rather forget?

318
Except Not

Write about two characters as they share in their first kiss, except... one of them is lying. One of these characters has been kissed before, and they're lying to their companion. Why would they do this? Who benefits the most from this lie? And what would the liar say if their companion revealed that they knew the truth all along?

319
Get a Room!

Write from the perspective of a character who is watching two people kissing. Explore the thoughts of this character as they witness the event. What does a 'kiss' mean to them? Have they ever been kissed themselves? Do they find their inspirations restored upon looking at that couple, or are they nothing but jealous? Also, what would happen if the kissing couple realized they were being watched?

320
Magic Kisses?

Write about a character as a stranger approaches them on the street. This stranger claims that they're 'cursed' and that only a kiss from the character would undo it. What does this character think about the stranger's claims? And, above all, is this character willing to kiss the stranger and see what happens?

321 - 324

Technology can be pretty helpful in most situations. The problem is not when technology fails, but rather when humanity makes the mistake. In the age of email and social media, what happens when we (mistakenly) broadcast our nastiest opinions to people we love and respect?

321
Reply to All

Write about a character who, after writing a very mean email about someone they dislike, happens to not only send it to said someone— but also everyone they know. What exactly did they write about? Who was it intended for? Is this character afraid that there will be severe repercussions to this email? And, now that the damage is done, what is their next course of action? Do they play it off as a joke, or accept they made a mistake and pray for forgiveness?

322
Trolls

Write about a character who discovers that someone they know has been saying very nasty things about them on the internet. Who is the person posting this? How does the character feel about it? What is their relationship with the person posting those nasty things? And, above all, is this a new development— or just the latest in a 'war' that has been going on for years?

323

It's a Secret to Everybody

Write about a character as they receive an email telling them that someone is going to start revealing their darkest secrets to the world. Does this character have reason to worry? What are they willing to do to stop this person from revealing their secrets— and is this person asking for something in return? What does this character do when, little by little, their secrets start being broadcasted to their family, friends, and coworkers?

324

Wikileaks Will Love This

Write about a character who sends an email containing very secret information off to people who were not supposed to see it. Who does this character work for: the government or a corporation? What terrible secrets have they exposed to the world? And now that the damage is done, what is their next course of action?

325 - 328

What is art without an artist? What is an artist without the money to get by? For how long can a person starve before they have to choose between their art and money? What if they chose both?

325

Poems for Sale

Write about a character who is selling poetry from a little stand on the side of the street. Describe their surroundings. What kind of people walk down that street? Do they stop and purchase poems— or is everyone too busy living their own lives? What about the poet? Explore the thoughts of this character as a person stops by their stand and purchases a poem. How does this make them feel? Do they see a bright future ahead, or is this the last nail on their coffin?

326

For You, it's Free

Write about a character who is selling poetry from a little stand on the side of the street, except there's one person they would never charge for their poetry. Who is this person? What is their relationship with the character? And, above all, if this character was starving and broke— would they dare charge this person for their poetry?

327

Poems for Trade

Write about a character who sets up a little stand on the side of the street with poetry, but they're not charging for it. This character asks people who walk by to leave a poem and take a poem with them in return. Why is this character doing this? What do they have to gain? Are they looking to help themselves or a stranger? What happens when a young person offers their stack of poetry in exchange for the whole lot?

328

Poems for Sale, Reversed

Write about a character who sees a 'poetry for sale' stand on the street. How does this character feel about this strange sight? Are they fans of poetry, or do they despise it? And yet, what drives them to walk up to that stand and purchase a poem? Do they see a part of themselves on the poet or in the words they purchased?

329 - 332

We are stubborn. We will make the same mistakes, time after time, regardless of what people around us tell us. It's only until the moment we want to learn that we do. Honestly put, people are dumb.

329
The Same Mistake, Every Time

Write about a character who continuously makes the same mistakes, time after time. What are they doing wrong? Does this have to do with their relationships, work, or lifestyle? Has anyone intervened in the past, and if so, how did this character react? What happens when they realize that, yet again, they've repeated the same mistake?

330
Can You Not?

Write about a character who happens to have a friend who continuously makes the same mistake. How does this character feel about their friend? Have they tried to help? After seeing their friend make that mistake so many times, have they lost hope that they will get better? What happens when their friend not only makes that mistake, yet again, but also endangers something that means a lot to this character?

331
If You Only Knew

Write about a character who continuously makes the same mistakes, except they are doing it on purpose. What reason do they have for making themselves look bad? Was there time when they didn't make that mistake on purpose? What would happen if they found themselves in a situation where they would either choose to make that mistake or save the life of someone who means the world to them?

332
Nobody is Perfect

Write about a character who continuously makes the same 'mistake,' except that, to them, it is not that big of a deal. Who has been telling this character that they need to change? Is their recurring mistake really something that needs fixing? Who benefits the most from this character changing: themselves or the people who demand this change? Could it be that sometimes... people are 'perfect' just the way they are?

333 - 336

Is there a situation as awkward as people around you forgetting your name? If it happens once, it can be chalked up to bad memory... but what if it happens more than once? What if it happens ALL the time?

333
What Was Your Name Again?

Write about a character who continuously experiences people forgetting their name. Did this start happening recently, or has it been going on for a long time? Why do people forget this character's name? Is this character really that forgettable... or could it be that there's something strange going on around them?

334
It Sure Ain't Sue

Write about a character who continuously experiences people forgetting their name. Not only that, but people also seem to forget their gender! Is this character androgynous, or are the people around them being rude? How would this character react if they met one person who *actually* remembered everything about them? Would they even believe something like that?

335

I'm Your Spouse

Write about a character who continuously experiences their spouse forgetting who they are. Is this character's spouse suffering a strange condition, or are they just playing games? How does this character feel about this, and why do they put up with it? For how long can you 'love' somebody who can't even remember who you are?

336

An Aura of Amnesia

Write about a character who continuously forgets a coworker's name. Is there anything unusual about the coworker— or can this character even remember what they look like? For how long have they known this person without actually 'knowing' them? And, worst of all, what happens when this character realizes that they're not the only one who forgets about this coworker?

337 - 340

Like the boy who cried wolf, a person can only lie for so long before they lose the trust of everyone around them. But… can there be more to this person than just a compulsive liar? What would happen if they needed to be truthful but nobody around them believed them?

337
Are You Calling Me a Liar?

Write about a character who has a reputation for being a big liar. Was this 'reputation' earned or simply given to them? Explore the thoughts of this character as they talk with someone dear to them. Does this person trust them, or are they careful to believe everything that comes out of this character's mouth? What would happen is something terrible was about to happen to the person dear to them— and only this character could warn them?

338
Well, I Ain't Calling You a Truther

Write about a character with a friend who is known for being a compulsive liar. How does this character feel about their friend's reputation? Do they see an element of truth in it, or do they think that it's all unfair? How does this character treat their friend? And, most importantly, do they trust everything their friend say— even if it's something quite strange?

339

The Liar's Club

Write about a group of friends who constantly lie to each other. What reason could there be for so much deception? Are they all trying to hide their hand, like they're playing a perverted game of poker, or is it all done for a good laugh? Explore a moment in this group, as all of the friends are out in public, enjoying a night out. Is it possible to find company and warmth around a bunch of liars?

340

Truer Than True

Write about a character who has an outstanding reputation for saying the truth, to the extreme that everyone around them trusts them without hesitation. How did this come to be? Did this character do something in the past to earn such a reputation, or are they simply that charismatic? What would happen if this character used this trust for their own benefit? After all, everyone believes what this character says without hesitation. It's not a lie if they don't find out, right?

341 - 344

There are only a few reasons why a child would be allowed to leave school early, but they all require some form of justification. A child can't just walk out the front door – but what if they did? What if a child walked out of school and nobody stopped them?

341
Leaving Early

Write about a young character as they leave school early. What reason do they have for leaving? What do their friends and teachers think of this reason? If there's a single person who would try to stop them, who would it be, and what reason would they have? And, what does this young character think about leaving school early? Are they really excited to leave– or would they rather stay at school than go to their destination?

342
No Chains to Bind Them

Write about a classroom of students as they stand up and walk out. What reasons do they have for doing this, and how did they all agree on taking this action? Are they just sticking it to 'the man,' or are they in danger? Explore the minds of the students, their thoughts and fears, as they walk out. And, worst of all, consider the point of view of the only student who does not walk out. Are they too afraid to make a choice, or have they already chosen for themselves?

343

Goodbye and Good Luck

Write about a teacher as they walk out of their classroom, intending to never return. What reasons do they have for doing this? Do they give a speech to their students before walking out the door— or do they offer no explanation except the look on their face?

344

Leaving Early, Reversed

Write about a young character as they walk back into their classroom, offering no explanation as to where they have been or why they left. Is there a reason for their secrecy? What about the people around this young character? Do they demand an explanation, or would they rather not know? People claim to always want to know the truth— but do they really?

345 - 348

There's something scary, and yet beautiful, about fireworks in the night sky. But does it make sense? Explosions and flame would've been magic to the primordial man. Why does this fire make us smile, when the same flame could easily destroy us and everything we know?

345
Fireworks

Write about two characters as they sit on a rooftop and watch the fireworks go off in the distance. What is their relationship and history together? Are they friends, lovers, or something else? Why is it that fireworks mean so much to them? Is it because fireworks remind them of something that happened a long time ago— or because the noise and flashes distract them from the problem they're too afraid to address?

346
Memories of the War

Write about a war veteran as they watch fireworks go off in the distance. Do the explosions and flashes remind them about the war? How does this character feel about being one of the 'lucky' ones who survived? And, above all, is there anyone they wish were able to watch the fireworks with them?

347
The Last Thing You Said

Write about two lovers as they watch fireworks go off in the distance. Explore their thoughts and their feelings. Unbeknownst to them, that is the last moment they are ever going to be together. What is about to happen to them, and what is the last thing that they say to each other?

348
Those are Not Fireworks

Write about a character as they hear and see explosions and fire in the horizon. For an instant, they think they're fireworks, but soon they realize they're something worse. What is it? Explore the moment when this character realizes what they're witnessing. What do they do next: are they frozen in fear, or do they start running?

349 - 352

Nothing lasts forever. All things that live must die, and everything that begins must one day end. Should it really be a surprise then that relationships, like all things, eventually wither?

349
The Friends Who Parted Ways

Write about two characters as they realize their friendship has run its course. For how long did their relationship last? Did it naturally come to and end, or did the actions of one party force the break? Explore both points of view. Who is really the person to blame? And, when it's all done, what is the one thing each character is keeping inside— and intend to never tell their 'ex-friend?'

350
Your Loss

Write about a character as they realize their once 'friends' have turned their backs on them without any explanation. Does this character have any clue their 'friends' had a change of heart? Is this character at all looking to find out the truth, or do they secretly believe that their friendship had run its course? What happens when their so-called 'friends' realize that this character is not at all impacted by their choices?

351

A War of Allies

Write about two characters as they realize their friendship has not only run its course, but that they now truly hate each other. What happened between these two characters, and why is conflict the only solution? Is there one person to blame for this all-out 'war,' or are both parties guilty of the same crime? Explore the reasoning of both characters, as they actively hate someone who they used to be their friend. And, above all, consider the following question: what would make them be friends again?

352

Between One Idiot and Another Idiot

Write about a character who realizes their two friends don't get along anymore, and that they may even come to blows at the slightest provocation. Explore the awkward situation of standing between two people one cares about, even though they don't care about each other anymore. Does this character try to 'fix' things, or would they rather cut their losses? If they had to choose a side, would they? But… are they even given a choice?

353 - 356

There are times when a parent must leave their child – though they may not always provide a reason. It's hard to admit, because everyone claims that their reasons are justified, but what of the child? Is it too much to expect them to welcome their parents with open arms after leaving them behind?

353
The Missing Parent

Write about a character as they come face-to-face with the parent who abandoned them when they were just a child. How has time treated both character and parent? Are they meeting by chance or choice? Who is the first to talk, and what do they have to say? And, above all, does it feel like a heart-felt reunion... or two armies meeting on the field of battle?

354
Not Family Anymore, but Strangers

Write about a character who finds themselves in a public place sharing a bench or table with a stranger. Unbeknownst to them, this stranger is the parent who abandoned them when they were only a baby. Explore this moment, and consider the thoughts of the character as they look at the stranger sitting next to them. Do they have any clue as to who this person is? What about the stranger? Has so much time passed that neither can recognize each other?

355
The Missing Child

Write about a parent as they come face-to-face with the child who went missing many years before. How has time treated both parent and child? Are they meeting by chance or choice? What is the first thing this parent does when they see their child; do they run to hug them or demand an explanation? Who suffered the most over the years: parent or child?

356
Who Returned in a Casket

Write about a character as they come face-to-face with the parent who abandoned them when they were just a child… except that said parent is dead. Explore the thoughts of this character as they find themselves at the funeral of a parent who was never there for them. What does this character feel about the people giving the eulogy? And, above all, how will this character find peace, now that the parent who abandoned them is gone forever?

357 - 360

To be an artist is to live at the divide between sanity and madness. To create and to spur new life from one's imagination is punishment enough... but what about the one thing no artist ever talks about? How does one face the reality that they only have the time to make one last piece of art?

357
The Last Song

Write about an artist as they struggle to make their very last piece of art. Explore the reason for their struggle. Are they trying to live up to past expectations, or are they trying to prove to themselves that they can do it? Who are they trying to please with this piece of art? If they're able to complete the piece, what do they see in it— have they created their last great work, or is it nothing compared to the art they made in their youth?

358
That Was Never Sung

Write about a character as they examine the last work of an artist who recently passed away. What is this character's relation to the artist? How is it this character, of all people, is the one looking over this work of art? What do they think of it? Do they consider this piece extraordinary in any way? And, what do they really see in this last work— what is it a reflection of? Was it all just art, for art's sake, or did it hold a special meaning?

359
Not the Last, but the First

Write about an artist as they *remember* the struggle of making their first piece of art. Explore their thoughts as they look back on the days of their youth. Were they an entirely different person back then? Compared to the years that would come, how does this character feel about their very first piece of art? Is there anything this character is bitter about, anything that they would change if they could go back in time?

360
That Defined an Era

Write about a character as they exhibit the last work of an artist who recently passed away. This piece of art, the last of its kind, is now famous for spurring a change in its medium. Explore not only the thoughts of the person presenting the piece but the thoughts of the people watching. What does that piece of art mean to them? And, if the ghost of the artist just so happened to be watching the exhibit, what would they think?

361 - 364

They say that in life we are all lost, and to live is to find our way out of the forest. But what if we don't consider ourselves 'lost'? What if... the forest was exactly the place we wanted to be?

361

Lost in the Forest

Write about a character who is continuously told by everyone around them that they're on the 'wrong' path. Is this character really 'wasting' their life? What are they doing that everyone around them seems so concerned? Explore the thoughts of this character as they, once again, face belittling from people close to them. Is there truth behind their words? And, worst of all, is this character going to change, not for themselves, but to finally silence their peers?

362

I Can Stop Whenever I Want

Write about a character who has a drinking problem, and it's no secret to the people around them. This character is constantly told that they need to quit drinking. How does this character feel about this? Why did they start drinking in the first place? How do they rationalize drinking their nights away? And, above all, are they interested in changing? They are the only person who can make the change, right?

363
Lost in the Forest, Reversed

Write about a character who continuously tells one of their closest friends that they need to change their lifestyle. This character strongly believes that their friend is 'wasting' their life. Is this true? How are this character's views on life different than their friend's? And, most importantly, what business does this character have telling their friend how to 'live?' Are they worried for their friend's safety, or is this just another way for this character to ignore their own problems?

364
Not All Who Wander are Alone

Write about a character who is continuously told by everyone around them that they're on the 'wrong' path... except this character is not alone. Explore a conversation between this character and a friend of theirs who shares the same lifestyle. What are they doing that everyone around them seems so concerned about? How do these characters feel about the path they're walking? Do they revel in going against the current— or are they simply looking for their own path? And, most importantly, what would happen if one of them decided to change?

365 - 368

What does it mean to become famous and gain the respect of countless people? What happens to an ego that is so blown out of proportion that one comes to expect adoration? Is there a dark side to this? After all... everyone wants to be a rock star, right?

365

The Celebrity II: Attack of the Fans

Write about a character as they're ambushed by a group of fans. Where are they, and what happened to this character's bodyguards? How does this character feel about being screamed at by rabid 'fans?' Could it be that this character... enjoys it? Does this character find joy in the maddened look of their fans? How would this character react if their fans didn't seem very excited to meet them?

366

Revenge of the Fans

Write about a character as they ambush their favorite celebrity. How did they manage to get past security, and how does the celebrity react? Is this character just looking for a picture and an autograph, or do they have something more important to share? And, above all, is this the first time these two people have met?

367
The Bodyguard

Write about a bodyguard as the celebrity they're supposed to be guarding is ambushed by a group of rabid fans. What's the first thing that this character notices? How do they feel about 'fans' in general? Examine their process as they attempt to rescue the celebrity. Does this bodyguard do anything that would get them in trouble? And, worst of all, are they to blame for the ambush in the first place?

368
December 8th, 1980

Write about a character as they're ambushed by a fan while they're alone. What's this character's reaction to being caught unaware? What is the first thing that comes to their mind when they realize the 'fan' has just pulled a gun out of their jacket? Explore the last moments of this character. Was a life of fame and fortune all that it was cracked up to be?

369 - 372

What is more terrifying to the young: the prospect of being drafted into a war they didn't start, or the idea that their selfishness may cost their country the war? Is there ever a time when the duty to oneself overrides the duty to one's country?

369
The Draft

Write about a character as they realize they've been drafted into the war. What is the first thing they do when they learn the news? How does this change their plans for the future? How do they feel about the draft; do they welcome the opportunity to help their country, or do they think they're going to become cannon fodder? And, above all, what dreams for the future did this letter shatter?

370
Mrs. Ryan

Write about a parent as they receive the news that their child has been drafted into the war— except they haven't yet told their child. Explore this character's thoughts as they consider their two options: telling their child the truth and sending them to the war... or not. The choice is in their hands, right? What is more important to this character: their child or service to the nation?

371

The Luckiest of All

Write about a character as they realize they're the only one out of their circle of friends who was *not* drafted into the war. Is there a reason for this, or was this character just lucky? How do they feel about their friends being drafted and about them being spared? What does this character do when their friends approach them, asking them if they got drafted as well?

372

I Volunteer as Tribute!

Write about a character as they volunteer to fight in the war. Why are they doing this? Do they seek to gain anything in the battlefield, or are they doing it to help someone else? Explore the thoughts of this character as they head to the front lines. Do they think it was worth it?

373 - 376

When faced with a terrible threat, all it takes is a second for a person to change. The selfless become selfish, and the selfish become selfless. Put a person in danger, and they will show you who they really are.

373

You or Me

Write about two characters as they struggle to survive in the wilderness. Their supplies are almost gone, and there is not enough for both of them to survive. Explore the thoughts of both characters as they face the harsh reality that if they *both* try to survive, they will both surely perish. Who is the first to speak, and what do they say? Do they face the reality or ignore it? Who becomes selfless and who becomes selfish?

374

All for One

Write about three characters as they struggle to survive in the wilderness. Their supplies are almost gone, and one of them is extremely ill. Explore the thoughts of all three characters as they face the harshest of all realities... that there may not be a way for any of them to make it out alive. What do these characters do? Are they all doomed?

375
And None for All

Write about a character as they struggle to survive in the wilderness. Their supplies are okay, but they have little to spare. What happens when this character finds another person struggling to survive? Does this character attempt to help this person, or do they try to take advantage of them? What has the wilderness done to this character— has it made them selfless or selfish?

376
Love and the Wind

Write about two lovers as they struggle to survive in the wilderness. Their supplies are almost gone, and there is not enough for both of them to survive. Explore the thoughts of both lovers as they remember the days when they first met. Only one of them can survive on the supplies they have. What do they do? And, worst of all, what would happen if one of the lovers was hiding the fact that they are pregnant?

377 - 380

What is a dream? Is it just our mind killing time in the night? Could it be there's more to it? What of the dreams that linger long after we wake up?

377
The Dream That Lingers

Write about a character as they share their strange dreams with one of their friends. What exactly happened in the dream, and what made it so 'strange?' How does the friend react to the retelling? Is there anything to the dream that hints it could be more? And, above all, what is the *one* element of the dream that this character has chosen to omit altogether?

378
I Dreamed a Dream

Write about a character as they share their life-long aspirations with one of their friends. What does this character desire, and why have they been unable to achieve it? What does this 'dream' mean to them? How does the friend react? Does this friend believe that the character can achieve this dream, or would they rather give them a reality check?

379

The Recurring Dream

Write about a character who experiences the same dream every night. What happens in this dream? Has this character ever told anyone about it? What would this character do if one day the events of the dream started unfolding in the real world?

380

The Butterfly that Dreamed

Write about a character who cannot tell the difference between the real world and the dreaming world. Explore their mind as they experience things that don't make sense in both realms. Is there a way for them to tell which world is the 'real' one— even then, do they really want to find out?

381 - 384

What are the odds of winning the lottery? Pretty low. What are the odds of two people winning the lottery? That's not chance, that's Fate.

381

Double Winner

Write about a character who wasn't the only person to win the lottery. How does this character feel about their luck? Explore their thoughts as they meet the other winner of the lottery. Do they know each other? Do they have a history? What does this character have to say to the other winner? What is the *one* thing this character is thinking but not saying?

382

Double Loser

Write about a character as they watch the results of the lottery and learn that, not one, but *two* people won. How does this character feel about losing the lottery yet again? Why are they so invested in this? Do they just want to get rich, or is there someone they need to help? Explore their thoughts as they read the results of the lottery. Are those… tears in their eyes?

383
Nothing to Gain

Write about a character as they reflect on the lottery they won several years before. How did it affect their lives? How did it affect the lives of everyone around them? Did their friends and family change? Does this character believe that the money changed them? If they could go back in time and prevent themselves from winning the prize, would they?

384
Super Duper Level Luck

Write about a character who wins every lottery they enter. How do they feel about this strange 'talent' of theirs? How has it changed the people around them? Does this character feel that *they* are lucky, or that *luck* is on their side? And, worst of all, what would happen if one day their luck simply… disappeared?

385 - 388

Where is the line between duty and obsession? What would push a person into breaking their own morals just to find the truth? What if there was no truth to find, but only fragments of a thousand little lies?

385
The Truth is Out There

Write about a character as they search for the answer to a question they've had for years. What are they looking for? Why have they dedicated so many years of their life on finding an answer? If they were to find the truth, who would benefit the most? And, worst of all, what would this character do if they realized there was no way to ever find out?

386
But I'm Stuck Here

Write about a character as they attempt to find the answer to a question they've had for years... except this character is confined to a room. Where are they, and who put them there? Explore the thoughts of this character as they desire, more than anything in the world, to escape that room and start searching for the answer. But— do they really want to find out the truth, or is this something they tell themselves to be at peace? What would they do if, all of the sudden, they were free?

387

It's For Your Own Good

Write about a character who has a terrible secret…
and also knows someone who has been trying to find out
their secret for years. What is this character hiding?
What's their relationship with the person who is trying to
find out the truth? What does this character do when the
person finally goes too far? How bad can a secret be that
one has to become a *terrible* person in order to keep it
secret?

388

The Detective's Triumphant Return!

Write about a detective who comes face-to-face
with the criminal they had been chasing their whole
career. Who is this criminal; what did they do to earn the
hate of this detective? Explore the mind of the detective as
they find out the truth once and for all. But— is there any
need for the truth? Who really benefits from the
conclusion of this saga?

389 - 392

Eclipse, like the sound of thunder, can strike fear in the hearts of men. It negates all natural laws. Light becomes dark, and dark gains light. But... could it be there's something else to it?

389
The Eclipse

Write about a young character who witnesses an eclipse. Is there anyone around to explain to them what it is? In their young mind, how does this character describe an eclipse? What does it mean to them? Does it scare them or excite them? What does this character do when they realize something else is happening at the same time as the eclipse? Are both events related? Is there reason to be scared?

390
Old Jenkins

Write about an old character as they try to warn people about the upcoming eclipse. What does this character know that no one else does? Do they have a real reason to worry, or is it all in their head? Is there anyone who believes this character? What happens when the eclipse comes? What would this character do if they realized they were wrong all along... and that something even *worse* is coming their way?

391
The Sky That Stopped Moving

Write about a character as they await the upcoming eclipse… except that it never comes. Explore the mind of this character as they experience no change whatsoever in the skyline. What is going on? And, worst of all, what do they do when they realize that no matter how much time passes— the skyline never changes?

392
Putting the 'Love' in Lovecraftian

Write about a young couple as they witness an eclipse… except something strange happens. Explore the thoughts of this young couple as an odd silhouette appears in the distance. What is it? Is it human or something… without a name? What does the young couple do when the silhouette starts walking closer, and closer, towards them?

393 - 396

It all began with a couple videos on the internet, and now you're famous. Thousands upon thousands of people want to know your opinion on everything. You make videos, you make money, and everything seems perfect – but has this 'fame' changed you?

393

Internet Famous

Write about a character who has gained a large following on the internet. How did they accomplish this? How has this 'rise to internet fame' changed their life? Are they still the same person they used to be, or has the eyes of a million subscribers bloated their ego? And, most importantly, are they more popular than videos of cats?

394

The First Video

Write about a character who has gained a large following on the internet, as they re-watch the first video they ever uploaded. How much time has passed? Do they feel that they've changed at all? If they could go back in time and offer their younger self one piece of advice, what would it be?

The Celebrity III: Reblog

Write about a character who has gained a large following on the internet, and while they're out in public they stumble upon a celebrity they adore. How does this character go on approaching the celebrity? What do they say? Do they introduce themselves by their internet 'persona?' And, ironically, what does this character do when they realize the celebrity is actually a big fan of theirs?

This is a Totally Serious Story Seed

Write about a cat who has gained a *VERY* large following on the internet, thanks to the videos its owner uploaded to the internet. What's so special about this cat; what makes it stand above the competition? How has this cat dealt with the fame? Is it still the same kitten it was months ago, or has the fame puffed its fur? And, most importantly, has this cat ever been on The Ellen DeGeneres Show?

397 - 400

What is the goal of a parent? Is it to prepare their children for the future, so they don't repeat the same mistakes they did? Why, then, do some parents wait until their very last moment to teach the most important lessons?

397
Last Piece of Advice

Write about a parent on their deathbed, their only child at their side. What is the history between these characters? What are they keeping inside that they would never voice? Explore the mind of the parent as they decide that the time has come to pass on their last piece of advice. Is this just what the child needed— or is it too late?

398
Last Piece of Advice, Reversed

Write about a child on their deathbed, their parents at their side. What is the history between these characters? How do the parents feel about outliving their child? Is it fair or is it just nature? And what is the piece of advice that the child offers their parents before their final farewell?

399

One Last Thing Before You Go

Write about a parent on their deathbed, their only child at their side— except that the parent is not who they say they are. What happened in the past, and how did that child end up with the 'parent?' Explore the final moments of the parent's life as they decide to tell their child the truth.

400

Passing the Torch

Write about a parent on their deathbed, their only child at their side. This parent, certain that they don't have a lot of time left, decides to pass on their last piece of advice to their child— except this is not 'their' advice. It was passed on to them, the same way they're passing it on to their child. Explore the moment where this parent repeats the cycle and passes the advice to their child. What does the child think about this 'torch;' is it nothing but history, or is it something they will pass on to their own children?

Thank You!

M. Kirin and friends hope that you have enjoyed this book.
Thank you for supporting independent authors and artists,
we could not do this without you!

"All the flowers of all the tomorrows are in the seeds of today."

Indian Proverb

More Books by M. Kirin…

RAVENSGEM

By M. Kirin

"Citizens of Iryport, we have gathered here today to witness a challenge of honor."

After two years of running, Lucian Wade has returned to Iryport. He left the city to escape the mistakes of his youth and now, he hopes that the past — and those he left behind — have given up on finding him.

But the past is relentless, and the person chasing him is not ordinary.

Johanna Kin, the most rich and powerful noble on the peninsula, is also Lucian's only childhood friend. She wants to see him— but she doesn't want to talk. Johanna calls a challenge of honor between her and Lucian.

A duel to the death.

Gadeean tradition demands that challenges be fought not with saber nor pistol, but with the blessings of the ancients. Within the veins of every Gadeean runs the black blood of The Mountain, and only they can ignite the power hidden in gemstones.

Separated from his allies, forced to fight for his life, Lucian clutches his ravensgem, and the power locked within.

"For too long I've been a victim of fate…"

M. Kirin presents **Ravensgem***, Book One of The Chronicles of Gadeen, a fantasy adventure novella about guilt and the consequences of one's actions.* **For more information, and a preview chapter, please visit: mkirin.com**

More Books by M. Kirin…

A SECRET NAMED SOPHIE

By M. Kirin

"To my dearest Niece..."

Sophie's uncle is dead. The letter informed her that Philip Spencer, the man who'd been both friend and guardian, died and left her everything he had.

She doesn't want to believe that her uncle is dead.

Hoping to find the truth, fifteen year-old Sophie leaves home and takes a train beyond the Smoke-Cities, to Jaycetown. In her heart, she hopes to find her uncle safe and the letter nothing but a cruel joke... except she's going to find *more*.

She will enter a mansion she didn't know existed, and find herself surrounded by photographs of people her uncle never talked about. Worst of all, a strange creature lurks in the darkness— but she can't turn back.

She is the last piece of the puzzle.

"I leave to you all of my earthly possessions."

M. Kirin presents **A Secret Named Sophie**, *the first in the Sophie Spencer Series, an upcoming novella about family and the lies that transcend time.* **For more information, and a preview chapter, please visit: mkirin.com**

WHO WROTE THIS BOOK?

    My name is M. Kirin. I live on the West Coast of the United States, and I like to pretend my friends and I have a sitcom. Whenever I'm not writing, or talking about writing, I'm probably *blogging* about writing.

    Okay, that's a bit of an exaggeration. I'm also an avid reader, gamer, and pixel-art maker. If you would like to know more about what I do, or want to stay up to date on upcoming releases, feel free to follow me on your preferred social platform!

Writing Advice Blog: *maxkirin.tumblr.com*
Website: *mkirin.com*
Twitter: *twitter.com/mistrekirin*
Youtube: *youtube.com/user/mistrekirin*
Wattpad: *wattpad.com/user/mkirin*
Patreon: *patreon.com/mkirin*
Facebook: *facebook.com/mkirinauthor*

For anything else, feel free to shoot an email to:

mail@mkirin.com

WHO MADE THE COVER?

Plaguesworth is…

A super evil scientist that resides from the darkest depths beneath the sewers of Moss Landing. He spends most of his time around his lab drawing abstract images and creating strange monsters to do his evil deeds (mostly just folding clothes).

Art Blog: *plaguesworth.tumblr.com*

Monster requests and *braaaaains* should be sent to:

plaguesworth@yahoo.com

Feedback

Did you enjoy this book? Do you have something to say? We would love to hear your opinion! Head over to the link below and leave a review:

bit.ly/400S1-review

We read all comments and consider all suggestions for future editions!

Full Index

Made in the USA
Middletown, DE
11 November 2015